BY THE
GRACE OF GOD

An Autobiography

Fr. Tom Uzhunnalil SDB

KRISTU JYOTI PUBLICATIONS
Bosco Nagar, Krishnarajapuram
Bengaluru – 560 036
India

BY THE GRACE OF GOD
AN AUTOBIOGRAPHY
Fr. Tom Uzhunnalil SDB

ISBN   :   978-81-936029-2-8
Price   :   ₹130/-, $ 8, € 7
Design & Print   :   Don Bosco IGACT, Kochi. Ph : 0484-2806411
Typeset by   :   Don Bosco IGACT, Kochi. Ph : 0484-2806411
Website   :   www.kjcpublications.org

Dedication

TO THE FOUR SISTERS OF THE MISSIONARIES OF CHARITY
AND 12 OTHERS KILLED BY TERRORISTS IN YEMEN ON MARCH 4, 2016

SR. REGINETTE

SR. JUDITH

SR. ANSELM

SR. MARGUERITE

PRECIOUS IN LORD'S SIGHT
IS THE DEATH OF HIS FAITHFUL
Psalm 116:15

PREFACE

Dear friends... My aim in writing this book is in the least to present myself as extraordinary. However, there are two reasons that made me chronicle my life experiences; especially my life in Yemen, life in captivity and the nearly miraculous release. The first reason is, I want to testify to everyone how God has been extraordinarily kind to me; how He kept me safe and healthy for 18 months of rather lonely captivity; how He intervened in my life in His own sweet time and ensured my release. Secondly, I want to thank the millions of people who prayed for me while I was in captivity. I believe and consider my safe release as the result of the intense prayers of all of you. Since my release I have been flooded with invitations from several quarters, by wonderful people who through their intense prayers made my release possible, to come to their place and share my experiences with them. In spite of my best of effort I have not been able to oblige all the invitations. This book is a way of reaching out to everyone I couldn't meet to thank. It is a testimony of my first-hand experience of God's protection. I hope and pray that it inspires you and enthuses your faith life in the Provident God.

My sincere thanks to Frs. Boby Kannezhath, Cyriac Thayil, Previnth Joe Tony, Dhaveedu Yesudas, Dominic Kaniyamtharayil, Prasad Kunnummel, Joy Kaippan and Br. Sumon Uzhunnalil for helping me in verbalising my experiences in the form of this book. My thanks in a special way to Fr. Joyce Thonikuzhiyil, the Provincial of the Salesian province of Bangalore, Fr. Jose Koyickal, the Vice-provincial and Fr. George P.S, the Economer. Special note of gratitude to Fr. Dominic Veliath, Fr. Punnappadam Thomas, Fr. George M.K, Bro. Shaji Nedumpurath and of course Kristu Jyoti Publications and Don Bosco Press, Vennala.

Fr. Tom Uzhunnalil sdb

TABLE OF
CONTENTS

A MOVING TESTIMONIAL OF FAITH AND A TIMELY REMINDER ON THE POWER OF PRAYER

For millions of people across the world, one of the happiest news items of 2017 must have been the safe release of Fr. Tom Uzhunnalil who was in terrorist captivity in Yemen for 557 days. I feel unable to recall any similar occasion in recent years when so many people, for so prolonged a period of time, so passionately, prayed for a specific intention such as the release of Fr. Tom.

As the Provincial of the Salesian Province of Bangalore to which Fr. Tom belongs, I was literally moved to tears on very many occasions seeing the intensity of the prayer-campaigns taken up by different individuals, families, parishes, congregations, Dioceses etc. The prayer-efforts towards the release of Fr. Tom was something extraordinary: Holy Eucharists, Rosary Campaigns, Night Vigils, Prayer Services, Fasting and Abstinence, Pilgrimages, Interreligious Prayer Meetings and Candle Light Processions. I personally had surrendered this situation to St. John Paul II and to St. Alphonsa. Fr. Tom's own youngest brother David made a pilgrimage of 1600 kilometres, on foot praying the rosary all through the journey for the safety and release of Fr. Tom.

Fr. Tom is personally known to me for close to 40 years; a very committed Salesian priest, an exemplary religious, a hard worker, a person with tremendous love for the poor and a man respected by all for his integrity and self-discipline. No one would have found fault with him if he had not gone back to war-torn Yemen. But being the only Catholic priest in Yemen with a religious visa, he felt duty-bound to be with his faithful in their hour of crisis.

In all the talks, interviews and formal/informal interactions since his release, never did anyone hear from him a word of anger or rancor. Is it that captive life was all fine and pleasant? I don't think so. Knowing Fr. Tom, I understand it as a matter of perception. He was living in the shadow of death. But mentally prepared for martyrdom, the thought of death did not really worry him. Being kept blindfolded and tied in captivity meant that he had lost the sense of time and count of days. With no contact whatsoever with the world outside, the same circumstances would have turned people insane; but Fr. Tom has not just survived it, but positively described the loneliness he was subjected to as 'time he got to pray and reflect'. He had physical ailments and health issues; but instead of being grumpy and complaining, he preferred to focus totally on graces and blessings he was receiving. Fr. Tom has repeatedly said that while he was in captivity he was fed well and on time. How many of us can enjoy a meal in an unknown enemy camp, blindfolded, not even sure of what exactly one was eating?

After the release of Fr. Tom, a microscopic minority was heard remarking; 'Why is Fr. Tom speaking good things about such wicked people, who killed the Sisters and others besides keeping him a captive for so long?' Fr. Tom is a priest after Christ who forgave His enemies. He is disciple of the Master who prayed for those who crucified Him. Those raising their eyebrows at Fr. Tom's capacity to forgive must realize that, every Christian is called to practice the same.

"I Thank God Almighty." These were the first words we heard from Fr. Tom Uzhunnalil as he addressed the public for the first time after his release. These are my genuine sentiments too as I present this autobiography of Fr. Tom Uzhunnalil, titled 'By the Grace of God' (1 Cor 10: 15). 'Grace' is a word that comes from the Latin word 'Gratia' which means to be grateful and thankful. I would like to gratefully remember our Holy Father Pope Francis, Fr. Artime Àngel Fernàndez our Rector Major, Fr. Francesco Cereda, the Vicar General of the Rector Major and Bishop Paul Hinder of the Apostolic Vicariate of Arabia South under whose jurisdiction Aden in Yemen comes, where Fr. Tom was serving. We also thank the Sultanate of Oman for their humanitarian way of acting in this particular situation.

I very specially thank Mr. Narendra Modi the honourable Prime Minister of India who always gave us the hope that Fr. Tom would be released and the Government was doing its best in spite of the inevitable hurdles that existed because of the lack of an embassy due to internal problems in Yemen. Very special thanks to Mrs. Sushama Swaraj the Honourable Minister for External Affairs, for assisting in the release of Fr. Tom. Whenever we met her, she gave us tremendous hope and authoritative assurance that Fr. Tom was alive and his release and the release of few other Indians were her topmost priority. We are also grateful to Mr. Pinarai Vijayan the honourable Chief Minister of Kerala, Mr. Oomman Chandy the Former Chief Minister, and all other leaders irrespective of political affiliations.

We are grateful to all at the CBCI, starting with his Eminence Baselios Cardinal Cleemis the president, George Cardinal Alenchery and Oswald Cardinal Gracias. It was so easy to approach them and they always guided us wisely. We are specially grateful to Bishop Theodore Mascarenhas the resident Secretary General of the CBCI office. He acted as the point of reference for us and as the one put in charge by the CBCI to liaison with the government. We are also very grateful to His Grace Bernard Moras, the Archbishop of Bangalore.

Our gratitude goes to all people of goodwill who were involved in the release of Fr. Tom in one way or the other; the entire world, irrespective of any possible differences, the dioceses and religious congregations that took up the release of Fr. Tom with so deep and faith-filled a prayer-campaign. The Syro Malabar hierarchy had added a new prayer during the prayer of the faithful for daily Mass with the intention of the release of Fr. Tom. I specially place on record the persevering prayerfulness, patient waiting and above all the mature Christian faith the Uzhunnalil family showed all through.

I appreciate the efforts taken by Fr. Tom Uzhunnalil to record his experiences in the form of this inspiring autobiography titled 'By the Grace of God'. This book is a classic testimonial to the truth that faith in God can see us through even in the biggest of calamities; at the same time a timely reminder to the world on the power of prayer.

Fr. Joyce Thonikuzhiyil sdb
Provincial, Salesian Province of Bangalore

I was
vulnerable,
but not
defeated.
I was anxious
but not
desperate.
I had worries
but never lost
trust in His
All-powerful
hands.

MY CHILDHOOD

Chapter 1

I really do not know where to start and what to write. Writing a book is something that I never imagined I would ever do; much less even attempt. But life, as it is full of surprises, sometimes lands you up in places and situations where you never imagined you would be and doing things that never occurred to you as you would do even in your wildest dreams. The purpose of chronicling my experiences is in no way to create an impression that I am a saint or superhero. In fact more than anyone else I can testify that I am far from all that. But I felt strongly impelled to write on my experience of the protection and mercy of God especially during the time that I was in captivity. May this prevent my falling into the category of the nine among the ten leapers in the gospel who never returned to thank the Master after they were healed.

Being a person more attuned to the technical side of everything around me, far more than the linguistic side, writing these lines was certainly rather a strenuous and tedious task. Many times I found myself in tears. I turned very emotional at several moments realizing how great a gift my life is. Looking through the past years, right from my childhood up to the present moment, I could find my God walking with me, taking care of me, not only in moments of joy but also in the most difficult situations of life. Even when there seemed no hope, He filled me with hope and courage. At times, when the prayers were seemingly unanswered, He held me close to Him. Often I wonder at those 557 days, when I was in captivity. I was vulnerable, but not defeated. I was anxious but not desperate. I had worries but never lost trust in His Almighty hands. My captors could have hurt me, but they never did. I could have succumbed to my high diabetes and hypertension. But the Lord did not allow that. While He gave me trials on one side, He strengthened me with graces on the other. I knew that the Lord would act in His own time, that His *Kairos* would surely come.

Ensuring the right alignment between our plans and God's will for us is very important to stay fulfilled in life. It calls for constant self examination. 'What does God want me to do in this given situation' is a question that all of us must constantly answer in our conscience.

There were moments when I asked God what my mission was. When I heard the gunfire and saw the Sisters and others fall, I thought the Lord was asking me too, to offer my life to Him in humble surrender. But then, I was taken a captive. Perhaps God didn't find me ready for or worthy of martyrdom. As the days in captivity went on and on, I was once again in perplexity as to what the Lord had kept in reserve for me.

But after I was released and reached home safe, I realized that my mission is to be a witness to the fact that THE LORD ALIVE HEARS OUR PRAYERS AND THAT HE WOULD SURELY ANSWER THEM IN HIS OWN GOOD TIME. I realize that I am a living proof that our God still loves us and cares for us. The One who knew me before I was born, formed me in my mother's womb and called me to follow Him closely, is ever at my side, strengthening me. My whole life has been an experience of His presence walking side by side with me.

My life began around six decades back in a lovely village of Kottayam District in Kerala, namely Ramapuram. This is a place which merits a unique place in the historical, religious, cultural and literary chronicles of India. Incidentally this lovely hamlet is the birth place of Malayalam literary giants like Ramapurathu Warrier (initiator of *Vanchippattu*, a popular folk art in Kerala) and Lalithambika Antharjanam (famous woman writer in Malayalam literature). A land of religious significance both for the Hindus *(Nalambala Darsanam)* and Christians (the land of several saintly people like Theverparambil Kunjachan, Paremmakkal Governador etc).

My house is situated towards the north of Ramapuram. We lived there in a little house, which was of course a house of prayer, affection and joy. I was the fifth among the seven children of Mr. Varghese and Mrs.Thresiakkutty.

Born on 18 August 1958, I was soon baptized at St. Augustine's Church Ramapuram. My eldest sister who accompanied me along with my Godparents (my uncle and aunty) still remembers the day when I was baptized at the old church at Ramapuram. Of course, the same church would later become my early school of vocation.

My father was a very affectionate man. I have always been impressed by his hospitality and care for others, a virtue which he tried to instil in each of his children. He was also a man of immense patience, so much so the only occasion I can remember him scolding me was on a day when I refused to join the evening prayers because I felt so sleepy that day. He demanded that I don't forgo my prayers. I was brought back from bed to sit with the rest of the family and be part of the evening prayers. Although I felt annoyed about it then, later on looking back at the incident I recall it as an occasion where I was taught valuable lessons on prioritisation. My mother explained to me and consoled me saying, "Chachan has beaten you because you refused to join in the family prayer." 'Even if you compromise on physical food, you should not do that with regard to spiritual food' was his clear policy of life. This value he stood for did leave a deep mark in my life.

My mother Thresiakkutty, was an exceptionally pious lady, whose simple devotion inspired me a lot. She was very kind in her dealings and was careful to bring us up as good Christians. She was brilliant at multi-tasking. She would run the kitchen, attend to every need of all the eight of us and still find time even to help out in the farm. Once when as a young boy I did something bad, she told me "Jesus does not like you to do that."

We were seven siblings: Mathew, Rosamma, Augustine, Mary, Joshy, David and myself the fifth, and I should say that a very close bond existed among all of us. As I look back, I realise that my parents had their own subtle strategies to keep us together. The elder sisters and brothers used to take care of us, the younger ones. I remember a time when my mom had to be away in the hospital for a prolonged period of time. We had to do all the chores by ourselves. My elder sister Mary used to manage the cooking. We were each given our share of work. My job was fetching water and taking care of my younger siblings Joshy and David. Though those were tough times, we grew up in unity and love.

Initially, I was put in Ramapuram North Lower Primary School for my primary education. But one day, I lost my mathematics table-book and the teacher punished me severely; so much so I refused to go to school the next day. But then, my father consoled me and took me to the school. Unfortunately, that day too, I was caned by the same teacher for something else. Thereafter, I did not go to that school again. I was sent to the nearby Lower Primary School run by the CMC sisters. There I was very comfortable, also because my grandmother's sister, Sr. Cathreena was there in that convent and school. I was very close to her and she used to show her special affection for me by giving me some sweets. Later on, as a priest looking back at the bitter caning that made me change the school, I have wondered at the ways God works. The pain of the cane was just temporary. It was God's way of leading me into the best of hands and hearts that would groom me.

Even small acts of kindness, concern and encouragement can have absolutely miraculous effects on children. One such memorable incident of a morale booster happened in my life when I was in class III. One day in class, Sr. Leena Manakkattumattom was taking class and she asked one question to the class, "why do the plants that grow under big trees have broader leaves?" The sunlight is less under big trees and bigger leaves will gather more sunlight, was my answer. Since I answered it correctly she was very happy. She gave me a small prize for my smartness and it was a picture of Infant Jesus, with a nice design stitched around it. I treasured it so close to my heart and felt so happy about it. As an adult, when I think of it now, I understand that it was her way of bringing me close to Jesus.

As I already mentioned, my parish church was St. Augustine's Church, Ramapuram. There were two churches side by side: the old church dedicated to St. Augustine, where the mortal remains of Bl. Kunjachan are buried and then the new church dedicated to Our Blessed Mother. Most of the liturgical services were held in the new church. This church had a beautiful sanctuary decorated with Portuguese art which evoked a lot of devotion in me. And of course, this church and the ambience here played a very special role in my vocation too.

I feel that for priestly and religious vocations to sprout we need three factors coming together. First of all, we need families that are rooted in prayer. Secondly, we need an ambience that encourages and nurtures vocations. Thirdly, we need living examples of joyful witnessing from consecrated persons. I consider myself very lucky at having had all these three factors around me. There used to be many missionaries who would visit our church, speak about the missions. Such narratives used to inspire me a lot and I believe the first seeds of my vocation have been sown by those missionary homilies that I heard. Our parish was rich in vocations and it has been a cradle of many saintly priests and religious. We had several Carmelite and Sacred Heart Sisters who used to be teaching Catechism those days and their inspiring lives had a deep and lasting impact in my young heart.

Those days, there was this holy priest who captured my attention with his saintly and zealous priestly life. That was none other than the later beatified Bl. Thevarparmbil Kunjachan (Bl. Augustine Thevarparambil). Even when he was alive, practically all the faithful considered him a saint. He was known for his mission among the harijans. He lived a life of poverty, simplicity and surrender to the Lord. I remember visiting him with my parents and seeking his blessings. Certainly, the person of this holy priest made me think of becoming one like him. When he died, I was in my ninth standard and I do remember attending his funeral. So much so, later in my life I would pray to Bl. Kunjachan, whenever I faced a difficult situation. Even during my days in captivity, I used to seek his intercession in a special way. St. John Bosco used to say; 'No priest will go to heaven alone. They will be accompanied by the many souls they saved for God'. I used to think of Blessed Kunjachan, visualising him entering into heaven with an army of people around him.

I was blessed with many priests in my family too. Two of my maternal uncles were priests; Fr. Augustine Vichatt and Fr. Abraham Aykkara. The former is still alive in Shanthivanam, Trichy, Tamil Nadu. Fr. Mathew Uzhunnalil, (fondly called as Achayan) who would later become one of the pioneering missionaries in Yemen, was my father's cousin. When I was a child, he was a missionary in Assam and the stories of the Assam missions I heard from him, would

My Parents Varghese & Thresiakkutty

Family Members

School Days

The Churches at Ramapuram, Pala

Blessed Thevarparambil Kunjachan

create in me a great desire to go to the missions in North East India. His arrival for holidays used to evoke the mood of a festival at home. He would speak a lot, about the missions, the struggles they had, the difficulties they had to overcome and the challenges they faced. He would visit the houses of all relatives and meet all of us. The figure of Fr. U. V. Mathew, had a deep influence in my life. So much so, it was after his return from Yemen due to old age and sickness, a mission which flourished because of his missionary zeal, I felt a divine mandate to take up the mission from him.

Later when I passed the 4th standard, I was put in St. Augustine's High School, Ramapuram. I was always just above-average in my studies. Often, I scored poor marks for languages, but fared well in the science subjects especially in mathematics. I used to have many boys as my friends, especially the children from around my house. We used to play around, go together to graze cattle etc.

My father being a hardworking farmer, we used to have early lessons in farming too. I remember, when my father used to prepare the bed for planting trees he would make each of us plant the saplings. And thus I too developed a special interest in farming. Once my maternal uncle Thommachan gave me some seedlings of vegetables especially of brinjal. I planted them all and they did yield very well. We had a lot of vegetables in those days and I carried the extra vegetables to the local market and sold them there. Earning a few rupees by the sweat of one's own brow was a huge thrill. Encouragement from parents towards such initiatives fuelled this enthusiasm even further.

The land I come from is known for rubber plantations. When I was in the 8th standard, we were having some old rubber trees near our house. During summer holidays, I took permission from parents and started tapping those trees. It was more a learning experience which meant that I get up early in the morning, do the tapping, collect the latex and get the rubber sheet ready each day. I must have continued it all through the summer. Selling those rubber sheets, we got thirty rupees and with that my father bought a goat for us. Later the number of goats in the fold would increase and when I was in my 10th standard we sold one of the goats for Rs. 50/-. A proud goat farm owner by then, using that money I bought a wrist watch.

During my high school days, the CML (Cherupushpa Mission League) was very active in my parish and I do remember going for mission collections from house to house. For the boys of my age at that time, it was of course fun time too; a time to visit the houses of friends and people we know. At that time, there was one of the assistant parish priests, Fr. Mathew Oozhakal, who used to help out the children with English lessons during his free time. I used to attend his classes regularly. As a teenager he was a great example for me on how to deal with children and take interest in their life.

It was when I was studying in class X that Fr. Philip Thayil sdb visited our school. Short in stature and full of life, he introduced himself as a Salesian priest. Although my own uncle Fr. U.V. Mathew was a Salesian priest, I hardly knew anything about the Salesian congregation. He met all the Catholic students studying in class X and asked if there was anyone who was interested in becoming a missionary priest. Though not emotionally very expressive, I felt very happy at that question. Becoming a priest was a desire that I had been nursing for sometime; but due to my own inhibition I had never told anyone. I promptly lifted my hand and then there were one or two others too. Fr. Philip called me to the office. There he spoke to me personally, asked me questions regarding my family and academics. After a chat of nearly 20 minutes he invited me to the Salesian vocation camp which was to be held at Don Bosco Vaduthala in Cochin. Later he visited my house too. It was a big time surprise for my parents. They seemed very happy when they came to know of my desire to become a priest and encouraged me wholeheartedly.

The academic year and the public examinations were over. The days of the vocation camp arrived. It was being held at Don Bosco Vaduthala. I was really excited about the very thought of the camp itself. There used to be a private bus by name KMS operating between Mundakkayam and Ernakulam via Ramapuram. I boarded KMS bus and reached Ernakulam. I reached Don Bosco Vaduthala around noon.

It was a green and spacious campus with a sprawling football ground and several buildings. There, for the first time, I saw a statue of St. John Bosco. But I knew nothing about him. There was also a statue of St. Dominic Savio. This saintly pupil of Don Bosco was very familiar to me, through books and narrations during homilies by priests. In fact, we had a statue of St. Dominic Savio in the wayside chapel at Ramapuram.

There was a large number of students from all over Kerala who had turned up for the camp. Even now I remember the kindness with which the Fathers treated us at the camp. The camp was packed with classes, activities, competitions etc. which kept us busy all the time. There was no time at all to think about home or feel nostalgic about the absence of parents and siblings. I simply enjoyed every bit of what went on in the camp. During the camp Fr. Thayil met me again, clearly explaining the challenges that lay ahead and clarifying the genuineness and firmness of my decision to join.

As we returned from the camp, we were all given a biography of Don Bosco. I read it and realised that here is a saint whose life and style I could easily relate with. After reading it, I circulated it among all my brothers, cousins and relatives and all who read the book and were inspired by the life and mission of Don Bosco.

After I came back from the camp, I prepared myself to join the seminary at Don Bosco Tirupattur. I felt extremely happy during those days as my desire was finally coming true. My father took me to Ramapuram and bought me all that was necessary for my stay in the seminary. My elder brother Augustine took me to the Terminal railway station of Wellington Island, Cochin to board the train with others to go to Don Bosco Tirupattur for the post SSLC course. And thus I joined the seminary.

While waiting at Ernakulam railway station, to board the train to Wellington Island Terminal station I noticed another boy of my age with the same size and colour of the suitcase and mattress bundle, waiting to board the same train. On getting acquainted with him, I realized that he too was travelling with me or rather we are both heading to the same destination for the same purpose. This was my first chance meeting with Manuel Mevada, now Fr. Manuel Mevada sdb, the rector of the Don Bosco institution at Irinjalakuda. ▪

Keeping
busy with
productive
and useful
activities
is a good way
of warding
off the
temptations
from devil.

SEMINARY DAYS

Chapter 2

The Salesian minor seminary was at Tirupattur in Tamil Nadu at that time. In June, 1975 I reached Tirupattur. It was the first time that I was travelling to a place outside Kerala, and so I was obviously very excited about it.

Tirupattur was a very small town then. The Salesians had started there a youth centre, school, college, etc; and were trying to improve the lot of the poor in the several villages around the area. For me it was an inspirational direct exposure to the way Salesians carry out their apostolate and live their consecrated life.

We were about thirty three seminarians in our batch. It was for the first time that I was living with friends who never knew Malayalam, friends from other States. Our batch consisted of seminarians from Kerala, Tamil Nadu, Andhra Pradesh and Karnataka. The very first challenge encountered was learning English. The only language of communication permitted in the seminary was English. Having studied in a Malayalam medium school, one can imagine the great blunders I must have made while trying to communicate in English. But we were helped a lot with very good classes and practical sessions on language learning.

Life with companions from other cultures certainly broadened our mental horizons. 'There are no strangers in here. There are only friends you haven't met. So, meet up everyone at the earliest and befriend them' was one of the pieces of advice we were given in the very first week we started our life together there.

Although I was staying away from home for a considerable period of time for the first time in my life, I can't recollect experiencing any homesickness primarily because the staff members were all very kind and supportive. We had classes in subjects such as English, Catechism, Don Bosco and Salesian life, Music, Good Manners and the like.

At the age of 17, when you are in a completely new set up, the mind is still very impressionable and I must confess that some of the Fathers I came across while I was a seminarian did leave deep imprints in my mind. There was Fr. K.C George, who was our confessor and teacher. It impressed me much, seeing him working in the garden and farm day in and day out, and spending much time in the chapel in the evenings. There were five regent brothers, Br. P. I. Thomas, Br. K. V. Sebastian, Br. Joseph Putti, Br. Thomas Augustine and Br. Camillus who were helping us out with everything which we were expected to do. I always looked up to them as role models of Salesian life.

In a matter of a few months, I learned and understood a lot of things about Salesian life.

Our time-table used to be very tight with hardly any free time. 'An idle mind is the workshop of the devil. Keeping busy with productive and useful activities is a good way of warding off the temptations from devil'. Our rector, Fr. Stephen used to explain the reason why the time table is normally a tightly packed one in every house of Don Bosco. Another highlight of life there, was devotion to Mary. 'Any person brought to the Salesian house is brought there by Our Lady.' The rector would quote the words of St. John Bosco and explain. A third thing that I specially experienced there was family spirit. There was always a lot of fun and joy in the community. This again was explained to us by the rector. "Sanctity consists in being cheerful. Salesians are specially called to work with and for youth. So we follow a spirituality that is youthful and one that appeals to the young." Quoting St. John Bosco, Fr. Rector told us.

Every programme organised was geared towards our self-improvement and training. We learned valuable lessons on working in teams through house system and sodalities. There were several forums to polish one's talents and skills.

Having been brought up in a family that was into agriculture, I specially loved the hours set aside for manual work. Here there were no more rubber trees to be tapped or goats to be grazed. But there was cultivation of vegetables, paddy, sugarcane etc; all of which I was keen on learning more about. In the heat of a basketball game once a playmate's finger hit my eyes and I had to be taken to the nearby dispensary on a cycle rickshaw. But I recuperated soon.

DB Tiruppattur: Journey to Priesthood Begins Here

Seminary at Tiruppattur

Perpetual Profession at Vaduthala

Diaconate Ordination at Kristu Jyoti College

On the Occasion of Ordination to Priesthood

As Advent season began we all started counting the days left to go home for holidays. It was nearly six months since we had come away from home. The days of holidays were looked up to with much anticipation and thrill. But unfortunately I had an attack of typhoid, and had to stay back in the seminary while all my companions went home for the holidays. I felt terribly dejected, but for a very brief while only. The Fathers and Brothers who were remaining back took such special care of me that didn't really miss my parents or dearones much.

After one year of initiation at Tirupatur, we were brought to Don Bosco, Vaduthala for the pre-degree studies. Though I had a liking for maths and science, at that time all of us had no choice other than arts subjects. I always enjoyed the technical side of things. So quite a bit of my spare time used to be spent on plumbing works. My interest and knowledge of plumbing began while I was in my 8th standard. My mother's brother, John Chelliyil whom we called fondly 'daddy' engineered to construct a water tank and did the plumbing for the water supply to my home in Ramapuram. He explained everything in detail and would involve me in fitting pipes and taps and valves. This experiential knowledge helped me in serving the community.

To expose myself to the Salesian charism and mission, on Sundays I was sent to Don Bosco Snehabhavan, Palluruthy in Ernakulam. It was a rehabilitation centre for street children run by the Don Bosco Fathers in collaboration with the Corporation of Cochin. This first hand exposure to the life of the underprivileged was a powerful eye-opener for me in several respects. It reinforced in me the relevance and scope of the ministry of Don Bosco: My work consisted in taking care of children whose parents had left them and gone, children rescued from the begging mafia and looking after kids whose parents are mentally challenged. Each child was a case by itself. I used to admiringly observe the Fathers there giving personal attention to every child, trying to get them back on track with life.

In the seminary at Vaduthala, along with our pre-degree studies, our training towards entering into the novitiate too continued. We used to have classes and conferences on it on a regular basis by Fr. James Adayadiyil, the rector. I vividly remember the visit of the great missionary from the north east, Bishop Mathai Kochuparambil sdb to our aspirantate and he enlightened us on the challenges and thrills of missionary life.

And now it was time to take a decision to go to the novitiate. I said to myself, "No turning back." After the completion of the pre-degree course along with my companions, I moved on to our novitiate house in Kotagiri, Tamil Nadu. It is a hill station in Ooty district of Tamil Nadu, a place abundantly blessed by God in natural beauty.

I had the privilege of having Rev. Fr. Antony Mampra, a man who is fraternal, gentle and soft spoken, as my novice master and Rev. Br. Joseph Elavanal as the regent brother in charge. Br. Jerome Das, Fr. J. Joseph, Fr. Shanu, and Fr. Zola my confessor, all influenced me much in my novitiate year. It was a very beautiful year. We were introduced to every aspect and challenge of Salesian life. Training was given to pray and meditate. Counselling and psychological assistance was provided. The rules and regulations of the Salesian

Congregation were thoroughly taught and doubts clarified. After a year, I made my first profession on 24th May, 1979.

After the first profession, I moved on to our philosophy college at Yercaud, another hill station in Tamil Nadu. During my philosophy studies we had Fr. Joseph Puthenkalam as the rector in the first year and Fr. Vincent Durairaj in the second year. Fr. Joseph Puthenkalam, being very paternal to all the brothers was fondly called "Pappa" and Fr. Vincent as 'Daddy'. My favourite subject in the entire study of philosophy was logic. It was a time when we were introduced into several extra-curricular activities as well. True to my nature, I was often behind the curtains, taking care of the technical side of things at all major events of the community such as theatrical performances, celebrations and cultural fests.

At the end of our philosophical studies before we dispersed for regency, we were given cassocks. The occasion of receiving the cassock was made all the more special by the presence of Rev. Fr. Egidio Viganò, the then Rector Major of the Salesian congregation who was on a visit to India. While we received the cassock, no family members were present, as that was not the custom. But back home they were overjoyed at the news and were praying a lot for me.

After receiving the cassock, I met Fr. Thomas Thayil, the then Provincial, and expressed my desire to work in the North Eastern missions. Fr. Provincial listened to me patiently and then narrated to me the need for personnel in the new centres opened in Andhra Pradesh. "You are interested in technical works. What about going as teacher and regent to St. Michael's Technical School at Guntur?" Although I had a great desire to be in the remote rural areas of North East India, I decided to set it aside for now and go to Guntur.

Thus I reached Guntur and had a very fulfilling year in the company of over 40 hostel boys who were undergoing technical training. Looking after them was a joyful experience. I learned a bit of Telugu too in the process. Besides, as the ambience was very conducive, I happily made use of the occasion to hone my technical skills.

In the following year, I was sent to Calcutta to do technical studies. I was moving out of South India for the first time. I was happy. My experience at Guntur had reinforced my thinking that if a poor youngster is given technical training a family can be rescued from poverty. Dealing with children who are school drop-outs, or those who couldn't afford long years of study, equipping them with a trade and making them self-reliant is a wonderful way of helping them out. I knew that the studies I undertook would empower me to help the poorest category of youngsters.

At Don Bosco Park Circus, Calcutta, I completed my City and Guilds studies in Telecommunication Technology and ITI Electronics. I carried on there in Calcutta as the tutor for the ITI wing for another year. Br. Charlie, Br. Paul, Br. Cyriac, Br. Mani, Br. Theophilus, Br. Andrew were all Salesian lay brothers who taught me and influenced me a lot there. Fr. T. P. George was my rector during these four years.

I made my perpetual profession at Don Bosco, Vaduthala in 1986. After having made the perpetual profession I moved on with my companions to Kristu Jyothi College, Bangalore where 4 years of theological and pastoral training is given before one is ordained a priest.

In the third year of my theological studies my elder brother Augustine passed away, leaving a vacuum in my family. I felt very sad at the loss of my brother especially because we were very close to each other. He was present with my father and Fr. U. V. Mathew for my first religious profession at Mount Don Bosco Kotagiri, on May 24, 1979. My good superiors and companions helped me a lot to overcome the sadness of loss and helped me move on.

Life in the last stage of formation was also eventful. Don Bosco Fathers had by then launched work in a big way for children roaming the streets of Bangalore. With the pioneers of this venture like Fr. Kollashany George, I too involved myself in this ministry for some time on Sundays. Having done technical studies, I was asked to be in charge of the recording studio in KJC. This meant spending sleepless nights on several occasions for the recording of audio cassettes. But I enjoyed this work a lot. During my holidays Fr. Thomas Myladoor, the then vice-provincial, having come to know of my technical bent, permitted me to learn computer.

On 21 May, 1990 I was ordained a priest. Inspired by the servanthood of Jesus my Master, I took as my priestly motto, "To serve and not to be served". Having been ordained a priest my first assignment was to be administrator at Don Bosco Vaduthala; where I myself had turned up for the first vocation camp more than a dozen years ago.

It does
not matter
how and
where I die,
but what
matters
is what I live,
serve and
die for.

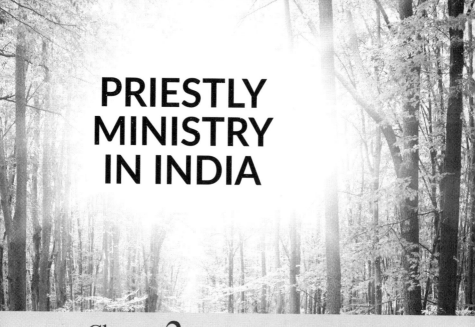

PRIESTLY MINISTRY IN INDIA

Chapter 3

If I were given another life, I would still want to be a priest. This is the sentiment that wells up in my heart and mind when I think of my life as a Salesian priest.

I am in the 27th year of my priestly ministry, which the Lord in His gracious design granted me to serve Him and His people. During these, almost three decades of my life as a priest, I was given the privilege to exercise the ministry in various roles assigned to me (Administrator, Vice-Rector, Assistant Parish Priest, Principal, and Rector) at different Salesian centres of mission (Vaduthala - 3 years, Kolar Gold Fields - 8 years, Hassan - 6 years, Bhadravati- 3 years, Yemen 4 years and, KJC - Bangalore - 2 months, Yemen 2.5 years) by my superiors.

After my ordination, my first assignment as a new priest was to be administrator at Don Bosco Vaduthala. This assignment evoked in me a certain feeling of familiarity with the place and people, given the fact that I had spent two years at Vaduthala while doing my pre-university studies during my formation years. Moreover, I was aware that Don Bosco Vaduthala, the first Salesian centre established in the state of Kerala, was a lively complex with a number of apostolic activities such as Centres of Youth Animation, Technical Institute, Schools, Parish and Pastoral Ministry, Social Empowerment and Out-reach Programmes, Awareness Programmes, Summer Camps for Children and Youth and the like.

As a young administrator of this ever-growing centre, what I experienced initially was the severe shortage of finance to meet the daily demands of various sectors. However, divine providence was never failing. Projects like the construction of the new ITI building, plans for a new church dedicated to our Blessed Mother (popularly known as Thattazhathamma), and the starting of a new English Medium School were also already underway supervised by different confreres of the community and the province. Fr. Joe Fernandez sdb was the Rector.

My task as administrator was to see to the needs of the confreres, day to day maintenance of the institution, procuring computers for the new Technical Institute, render spiritual and sacramental assistance at our semi-parish. On completion of my one year service at Vaduthala, I was tipped to do CTI (Central Training for Instructors) at Kurla, Mumbai, which finally did not materialize, since I did not manage to get admission. Subsequently, I was asked to continue at Vaduthala as the vice-principal of the Technical Institute.

My involvement at the Technical Institute consisted in collaborating with Bro. Chacko Nettickattil sdb in successfully obtaining NCVT (National Council of Vocational Training) recognition for three of the ITI Trades (Electronics, Electrician and Machinist) and taking classes for the students of electronics who numbered around thirty. My ministry in this capacity lasted two years.

After the three-year-stint at Vaduthala (May 1990 to May 1993), my next appointment was to be at Kolar Gold Fields (KGF). In 1993, the then archbishop of Bangalore, Most Rev. Alphonsus Mathias, wanted the Salesians to take up any one of the seven parishes in KGF and made his proposal to our Provincial. The then Provincial Superior, the late Fr. Thomas Myladoor, and his council, after due discernment accepted the offer and chose St. Joseph's Parish, Susaipalayam, KGF.

One of the primary criteria in the selection of this parish was the difficult economic and social conditions of the people of this locality. The parish of St. Joseph's Church, Susaipalayam, along with an Upper Primary School (adjacent to the parish campus) and a Technical Institute (Royal ITI, located at Ashoknagar, Robertsonpet) were handed over in perpetuity to the Salesians of Don Bosco on 7th October (Feast of Our Lady of the Holy Rosary) 1993 by His Grace, Alphonsus Mathias. Fr. C.A. George of happy memory was appointed to be the In-Charge of this new mission as Parish Priest, Manager and Rector. My designation was to assist Fr. C.A. George in pioneering this Salesian mission at KGF, besides being the Principal of the Industrial Training Institute (ITI) and seeing to the administration.

I reached our parish at KGF on 3rd June, 1993 and spent the next eight years there, until May 2001. Since my stay at KGF was longer than in other places where I was asked to serve and furthermore, since it was a pioneering mission, I shall narrate my experiences in KGF a bit more elaborately.

While I found myself in a new surrounding with insufficient knowledge of the local language (predominantly Tamil), I must acknowledge that the cordial welcome and whole-hearted support of Fr. Gregory who was the acting parish priest, his brother Prof. John, the assistance of the Parish Priests and Sisters of St. Joseph of Tarbes, the support of the local leaders like Mr. Dass Chinnaswami, Mr. Thomas, Mr. Mathew, Mr. Michael, the warm reception by the parishioners and other new friends of the locality were of great help and encouragement.

Since we had to shift the Royal ITI from Ashokapuram (which was five kilometres away from St. Joseph's parish), my attention in the first few months was concentrated on studying the various possibilities for its temporary relocation, until we were able to find a location of our own. In consultation with Fr. Mariapragasam, the then parish priest of St. Teresa's church, KGF, temporary arrangements were made for the classrooms at the church premises (situated about three kilometres away from St. Joseph's).

Another piece of land with a small shed (Teresian Vocational Training Centre) at Irudayapuram village, situated close to St. Teresa's church campus was handed over to us for use as practical labs. In a few weeks time we were able set up the class rooms and labs and shift the machinery to the new location and begin classes; in the meanwhile appointment of teachers and admission of new students were also undertaken. Until the arrival of Fr. C.A. George who was away on mission-preaching in the US, I was the only Salesian residing at our presbytery at St. Joseph's.

One night during those initial months, (18/08/1993), while I was still alone in the presbytery, I had the experience of being locked up in the presbytery from the outside, (which I came to realize only in the morning when the sacristan came to alert me), by some thieves who broke open the church and the tabernacle, stealing the sacred vessels after leaving the Sacred Hosts bundled up in a corporal beside the tabernacle. Probably, the culprits thought that the gold and silver-plated sacred vessels were of pure gold and silver. We never managed to recover them even after the police were intimated and investigations undertaken. However, this experience did not trouble me or make me shift my focus from the mission at hand.

With the arrival of Fr. C.A. George (11/09/1993), plans were mooted to take up and address the economic and social challenges of this new mission and the pastoral needs of the faithful. The first-hand preparatory survey and study revealed to us that poverty, poor housing, acute unemployment due to the impending closure of the mines at the well-known Kolar Gold Fields, lack of employment opportunities, social stigma, unskilled labour force and the inadequate educational and technical qualification of children and youth, were areas demanding our immediate attention and intervention. It was clear to us that infrastructure and land were essential to envisage any substantial developmental projects. The land for the construction of an

ITI building was an urgent need. The land surrounding our parish campus belonged to the BGML (Bharat Gold Mines Ltd), the Industrial Estate with various units of production and the people of the village respectively.

Due to the non-feasibility of acquiring land in the vicinity of our parish, the archdiocese came forward to help us and allotted its two-acre vacant piece of land at Irudayapuram for the purpose of setting-up the ITI. This plot is located about three kilometres away from our parish and within the jurisdictional territory of St. Teresa's parish. The late Fr. Thomaiyar was the then parish priest of St. Teresa's. A bigger shed was purchased (Kavitha Industrial Unit later renamed Don Bosco Annexe) at the Industrial Estate with the intention of conducting the practical classes of the ITI students and to provide employment opportunities to people by starting small scale productions. This shed was in the vicinity of St. Joseph's parish. The theory classes for the ITI students continued to take place at St. Teresa's premises.

I must acknowledge that, Fr. C.A. George, through his whole-hearted involvement, took a keen interest in the all-round development of the people. Through his personal contacts, daily visits, meetings with different groups of the villages, animation programmes, and involving people's active participation at all levels, he reached out to everyone. In order to address the various needs without undue delay, concerted efforts were also made to seek the aid of both governmental and non-governmental agencies. Many of these initiatives were by Fr. C.A. George and my duty was to execute them.

Permit me to narrate some of the developmental initiatives we were able to undertake and execute gradually in the next few years. With a view to skilling unemployed women, training in gem-cutting and tailoring were initiated in the parish campus with the help of donors like Mr. Tom Pot. Trainers were appointed and marketing possibilities for the small-scale productions from these ventures were identified. Women's Self-Help Groups and small-scale saving schemes were launched with the assistance of BMSS (Bangalore Multi-Purpose Service Society). As part of parish animation, the movement called 'Movement for a Better World' (with the help of Fr. Henry and his team from Kottar Diocese) and the formation of *Anbiyams*/Basic Christian Communities were also introduced in the course of time.

With the timely intervention of our developmental office, Bangalore Rural Educational and Development Society (BREADS), we were able to start the CFCA programme (Christian Fund for Children and Aging). This scholarship and charitable scheme would come as a providential help to very many poor families and especially in the education of the children. Looking back we can say that this project has enormously contributed to the promotion and transformation of social, health and educational conditions of the children, youth and the elderly of the parish.

During the early years, the accommodation facilities of the Salesian community at the presbytery were so minimal that even up to ten Fathers and Brothers had to share a small room for their stay with just a single bathroom cum toilet adjacent to the presbytery. The safety of this room was such that, one fine morning, these confreres woke up to the disquieting experience of having a strange guest resting on top of the bed sheet they were sharing to battle the cold: a five-foot highly venomous snake. The few confreres who woke up to this spine-chilling realization had the presence of mind to throw the snake out of the room along with the bed sheet, without waking up their other sleeping companions.

While still searching for donors to fund the proposed ITI building, divine providence came to us in the form of a housing project. Over a period of about five years we were given the assistance by an agency of German Doctors, (through the instrumentality of the then Mission Procurator, Fr. Thomas Vailatt sdb), to construct about sixty new houses, (each measuring 500 sq. ft.) for the most deserving people of the parish. We knew that the process of selecting the most deserving beneficiaries was not going to be an easy task, since the vast majority of the people of the five-hundred plus families of the parish were on a par when it came to the question of housing facilities. Therefore, we thought it would be wise to execute the selection process in a participatory way by asking the zonal family groups/*anbiyams* of the parish to prepare a list of the most needy on a priority basis which would be studied and evaluated further by us.

Once the most deserving ones were identified in a consensual way, a unit consisting of six houses each was taken up at a time for construction. Fr. Gregory was kind enough to spare one of his masons working at St. Mary's school. The members of the families benefitting from the housing scheme were expected to contribute by way of manual labour as assistants to masons (not only in the construction of their own houses but also in the construction of the other five houses of the unit to which they belonged). We adopted this methodology for the following reasons: 1) to speed up the construction process and to reduce the expenses; 2) to make the beneficiaries own up the project/ scheme by their active participation (like digging the foundation and assisting the masons as full-time helpers), and 3) to inculcate among them a collaborative spirit and mutual co-operation. The families selected for the housing scheme were obliged to commit to these demands, even though at times it required much patience, energy, firmness, dialogue, understanding and time. Implementation and supervision was largely entrusted to me by Fr. C.A. George.

Based on the experience of seeing the construction works supervised by Fr. Jose Vettom at our Salesian centres at Don Bosco Vaduthala and Don Bosco, Mampetta, I got the idea of trying out a few experiments in regard to the construction of houses, namely: 1) the manufacturing on our own, at our premises, the solid blocks required for the house construction, for which the technical know-how was obtained from Mr. T.J. Thomas' Gina Engineering Company (A mixing machine was purchased and a mould was also prepared, for this purpose); and 2) the welding and fabrication of truss, frames for doors and windows at our industrial unit.

Fortunately, these experimental initiatives proved to be successful and they eventually helped at least a few persons in developing additional skills and also to find a part-time employment and livelihood. While the housing project was still on, we received the welcome news from BREADS, about the sanction of the ITI building project. On 14th December,

Kolar Gold Fields

A Mine Field at Kolar Gold Fields

ITI Building Construction in Progress at Kolar Gold Fields

In Front of the Newly Constructed ITI Building

Construction of Houses for the Poor

Don Bosco ITI, Hassan

1996, a few days before the laying of the foundation stone for the ITI., my beloved father passed away. The building site was blessed and the foundation stone was laid on 24th December 1996.

The success of the manufacturing experiments helped us to replicate these and few other new ventures, when it came to the construction of the Technical Institute. Since my educational qualification was in the field of electrical and electronics and since there were technically qualified confreres like deacon George Mathew, Br. K.C. Mathew, Br. Jose, Br. Johnson, Br. Jimmy, Br. Thomas P.D, Br. Joachim, and others with the assistance of the licensed contractor named Mr. Jansidass, the electrical and electronics works of the ITI building were done by the Salesians themselves. The fabrication of cots (with the help of Mr. Michael), grill works, tables, desks, benches and other furniture for the technical school, residence and stay home for boys were also taken up under direct supervision.

All these works kept me constantly occupied and also brought me in close contact with very many good and helpful persons from all walks of life and from different religious and social backgrounds. In this regard, I must acknowledge the leadership and commitment and dedication of Fr. C.A. George, who made a great impact as a passionate missionary-pastor in the parish as well as all around KGF. In November 1997, while attending the course for missionaries in Rome, Fr. C.A. George was diagnosed with cancer.

In the wake his illness, there was a move to appoint me as the Rector of the community at KGF., which finally the

Provincial did not insist with me, knowing the nature of the various works I was already engaged in. Fr. I. Raj from Chennai province was kind enough to render his services for a few months in the pastoral ministry. In May 1998, Fr. C.A. George was transferred to Don Bosco Vennala as Rector, where he would breathe his last on 25th April 1999, succumbing to advanced stomach cancer from which he had been suffering for a considerable period of time.

In 1998, Fr. Thomas Augustine, a man with a large heart for the poor, would succeed Fr. C.A. George as Rector, Manager and Parish Priest. While the ITI and housing projects were still on, a few other developmental works were also under taken. In the place of the old shed for gem-cutting, a two-storeyed building was put up adjacent to the presbytery and with the help of the archdiocese, the roofing of the Upper-Primary School building was replaced with zinc sheets.

I recall with gratitude the constant assistance of our Provincials and their Councils, my community members, the project office of BREADS, the Parish Priests of the nearby parishes, the sisters, officers at the various government departments, the ITI Staff, Parish Council and very many friends. Much of the work was executed seeking the help of persons like Prof. John (the brother of Fr. Gregory), Mr. Michael, Mr. Mathew and Mr. Thomas, (of the Theruvamkunnel family), Ijaz Bhai, the Rotary Club, business people (like Bharat Hardwares, Matha Frames, Mahendra, KGF Mills), local leaders etc.

The ITI building was blessed on 4th September 1999 by Most Rev. Ignatius Pinto, the Archbishop of Bangalore, and inaugurated by Rev. Fr. Mathew Maruvathrail, the then Provincial of Bangalore. The stay home for boys was inaugurated by Mr. P. Chamberlain, the representative of the agency Mondial that had funded the stay home. The housing scheme was practically completed by May 2001.

Simultaneously managing the ITI as Principal, supervising the housing scheme, monitoring the construction of the ITI and other developmental schemes besides the pastoral ministry (both in the parish and nearby institutions) were both fulfilling and extremely demanding. Undoubtedly, the presence and active involvement of several Fathers and brothers would also contribute to the shaping up of our apostolic presence at KGF. I must admit that, amidst this hectic schedule, I could not do full justice to the students by way of my fulltime presence at the ITI. This fruitful ministry at KGF would be officially completed in May 2001 with my transfer to Don Bosco Hassan.

My appointment at Don Bosco ITI Hassan meant that I had to fulfil the twin roles of Rector and Principal. Don Bosco Institute at Hassan was already an established centre by now. Hence, except for the ITI related engagements, it was quite different from the pioneering mission at KGF. With the experience at KGF, it was possible for us to take up with greater confidence similar initiatives at Hassan in regard to fabrication and production. We found that the facilities available in our ITI were suited to initiate some fabrication and small scale production works. Added to this, this exposure in fabrication and production would help also the students in their skill training which could equip them to have a better chance in finding employment. Moreover, it was envisaged that this initiative would fetch some income in meeting the expenses of running the ITI and boys' hostel. With these intentions in mind, we took up the fabrication of desks, benches for nearby schools and institutions, which to a great extent proved to be meeting our original intentions.

On completion of my first year at Hassan, I was relieved of the responsibility of Principal and Fr. Raju Philip was appointed Principal of the ITI. Now, having to fulfil only the responsibility of Rector, I could afford to render pastoral services to the nearby religious communities and institutions by way of preaching recollections and administering the sacrament of reconciliation. I could also focus much attention on taking up more orders for production and fabrication.

Besides the ITI, we also had a farm at Kandalli, which the province had purchased in order to maintain and develop the ITI. With the help of the province we were able to dig wells and begin developing the farm. Since, Fr. Jaimon, the administrator, was interested in agriculture and farming, much attention was paid to the cultivation of the land.

On completion of my first term (three-years) as Rector, I was asked by the then provincial, Fr. Jose Kuttianimattathil to continue for another term. In the meantime, Fr. Raju Philip was appointed Rector and Principal at KGF., and Fr. Roy Isaac came as his replacement. With the completion of the second-term as Rector, I was due for a transfer according to the normal practice in our settings.

My ministry at Hassan lasted six years in all. I acknowledge that I was able to do what I could in the company and with the support of my own confreres, staff, students, priests and sisters of nearby institutions, friends and collaborators. Looking back I can say that I had a fulfilling and pleasant stay at Hassan (2001-2006).

My next assignment was at Don Bosco, Bhadravati, situated in Shivamogga district. In 1994, at the invitation of the bishop of the diocese of Shivamogga, the Salesians had already taken up the parish at Paper Town and established a Technical Training centre at a property indicated for this purpose by the diocese.

My ministry at Bhadravati consisted in serving as the Administrator and helping out in the Technical School. As far as the Technical School was concerned, there was a proposal from the provincial council to study the possibility of upgrading it to a Polytechnic. While Fr. Sunil Orathel was busy seeing to the running of the Technical School, I took up the task of studying the possibilities and obtaining the necessary approval from the technical department for this upgradation.

As part of the procedures, I had to approach the governmental office of the technical department in Bangalore to present the credentials and necessary documents. On one occasion, after my visit to the office at Bangalore, I had my lunch in one of the restaurants close to the City Bus Stand at Majestic. On my return after the hand wash, I came to the realization that my suitcase containing all the documents (related to the Technical School, land, bank, etc.,) was missing and nowhere to be traced. Almost desperate, I informed the Bishop and my community at Bhadravati. After making a police complaint, I returned to Bhadravati empty-handed. A few days later someone from Bangalore contacted us informing that a suitcase was found in one of the apartments near Gandhinagar, close to the Majestic Bus Stand. Fr. Edward Alapurackal, the Rector of Yuvodaya, (Centre run by Don Bosco Fathers to rescue and rehabilitate children on the streets of Bangalore) at Gandhinagar, close to the Majestic Bus Stand) was contacted and the arrangements were made to bring the suitcase to Bhadravati. On receiving it, I found that except the umbrella, all the documents were left intact. Probably, those who stole the suitcase and later abandoned it finding that there was no money or anything really worth in it to take away.

The effort to convert the training centre into a Polytechnic did not materialize, since the application was not approved. Our next attempt was to obtain an NCVT recognition for ITI. In the following year, application for NCVT recognition was made and we would successfully obtain the approval.

It was when I was about to complete my third year of service at Bhadravathi (2006-2009), that the then provincial superior Fr. Thomas Anchukandam sent out a circular to all the confreres of the province of Bangalore, inviting those willing to serve in Yemen (a mission entrusted to the province of Bangalore by the Congregation since many years) to let him know their mind. Heeding to an inner call, I expressed my readiness to the provincial to serve in this mission and eventually I was assigned for the same.

To conclude, I believe that God has a plan for each one of us. The experiences in my life as a priest prompt me to say that I must always remain open to God's plans in my life. I have no fear in venturing out into the mission of the

Lord with the blessings of my superiors. Serving the Lord by serving others has been the motto of my life. I thank the Almighty that with my own little efforts I could serve my brothers and sisters to contribute to their lives.

I firmly, believe that in this journey of life as a priest, the most sustaining elements were certainly the grace of God, the intense prayers of my beloved parents and family members, the accompaniment and support of my own superiors, confreres, prayers and support of the people of the parishes, staff, students, benefactors, friends of all religions, and so on.

Thanks to these innumerable blessings; I never had to face crises or any sort of accusation as far as living out my priesthood was concerned. One thing that I am convinced of now, more than ever, is that praying for one another and serving one another can work wonders. I believe, that the purpose of our life is to reach our ultimate goal, i.e., God. It does not matter how and where I die, but what matters is what I live, serve and die for. When I look back on my own life as a priest, I can humbly say that I have never regretted about this gift and task of vocation to the priesthood and if I were to be given another life, I would love to be a priest again.

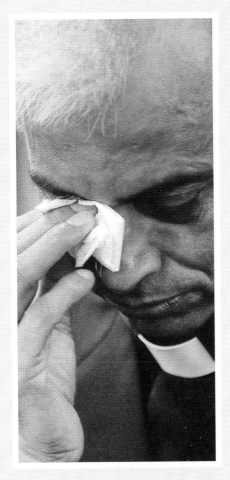

Such
incidents will
not deter us.
Our strength
is in Christ
Jesus. So long
as these poor
people would
need our
help we will
continue
our service
in Yemen.

MISSIONARY LIFE IN YEMEN (2010-2015)

Chapter 4

By May 2010, I completed three years at Don Bosco Bhadravathi, the paper town of Karnataka. Since my ordination in 1990, for the most part I was in different technical institutions, imparting training to poor youth. By now, I had completed 18 years at a stretch in four different technical training institutions. It was obviously a fulfilling ministry.

I must have taught nearly two thousand youngsters during the course of these 18 years. Invariably everyone of them was from financially very poor families and so employment for someone from the family meant that a family has been saved from economic crisis. It was always a joyful sight to see them standing on their own feet and supporting their families. Many who were employed in other major cities or outside the country, would make it a point to pay a visit and renew the friendship when they came for holidays.

As I have mentioned earlier, I enjoy the technical side of things more than the linguistic side. Since I have been dealing with youngsters, technical training, classes, placements, machines etc. for such a long period of time, I thought of requesting Fr. Provincial for a change of experience. I looked forward to a ministry where I would get to spend some more time in prayer and pastoral ministry.

In January 2009 we had a new Provincial Fr. Thomas Anchukandam in office. A very learned man, he was earlier my own professor of Church History at Kristu Jyothi College, Bangalore. He knew me well. As part of his task of giving animation and guidance he came around the different Don Bosco institutions to meet everyone and give suggestions and directions. When he came to Don Bosco house Bhadravathi I met him and mentioned to him that I was completing my third year in office as administrator in Don Bosco ITI Bhadravathi.

"I have been in the technical training centres for quite some time. I would love to have a change of experience for a brief period", I said.

Fr. Provincial was very understanding. "That's a reasonable request. Do you have any suggestion?" he asked. "If its fine with you I am ready to go to Yemen as a missionary to look after the parish and to assist the Sisters of Charity who are working there".

"Let me see. I shall keep your suggestion in mind when I prepare the next transfer list." He said smilingly. The transfer list was still four months away. But I felt happy that he took note of my desire to have a mission experience, something I have been longing for since my days as a student of philosophy.

Now, why did I then suggest to the Provincial that I am interested in going to Yemen as missionary?

There are several reasons. There were a couple of times in the past especially after my philosophical studies when I expressed my desire to be a missionary, but was told to wait for more opportune time as the new Province of Bangalore, comprising the states of Kerala and Karnataka and Andhra Pradesh had shortage of personnel in the different institutions, especially in the technical training centres, which were catering exclusively to poor youth by skilling them in different trades.

I need to say something about Yemen and the Mother Teresa Sisters who work there, before I say anything more on why I opted to go there.

Yemen, formally known as the Republic of Yemen, is an Arab nation in Western Asia at the southern end of the Arabian Peninsula. In fact with a coastline that stretches over 2000 kilometres, it is the second largest country in the peninsula. Yemen, a developing country and perhaps the poorest country in the Middle East now, has a very rich past. One etymology of Yemen derives from the word 'Yumn' meaning 'felicity' as much of the country is very fertile. The Romans called it 'Happy Arabia' (Arabia Felix) as opposed to 'Deserted Arabia' (Arabia Deserta). The civilization of Yemen according to some studies dates back to 5000 BC.

The political history of Yemen leading up to the present turmoil is a rather long narrative and I shall talk about it after I narrate my ministerial experience there.

The starting point of the ministry in Yemen was an invitation from the government of the Republic of Yemen to St. Teresa of Calcutta, then popularly known all over the world as Mother Teresa. The congregation of the Sisters of Charity founded by St. Teresa of Calcutta was setting new benchmarks in compassionate care of the poorest and the most needy across the world. Mother was getting invitations from all over the world to extend her work to their countries.

In 1973, the government of the Republic of Yemen invited the Sisters of Charity founded by St. Teresa of Calcutta to open their institutions in Yemen to look after the helpless destitute there. Yemen was a country that did not permit the practice of any religion other than Islam. This stood as a stumbling block for Mother Teresa to accept the invitation. Mother pointed out to the government that the source of strength for all their work is the Eucharist, and so in consonance with the policy of the congregation, the Sisters of Charity would come and work in Yemen, provided Catholic priests are allowed in places where the Sisters work. They wanted the presence of priests to administer Sacraments for them and to give them spiritual guidance. 'It is the spiritual energy that sustains us and helps us to carry out our ministry with love and joy,' Mother wrote to the government.

The government of Yemen after discussions agreed to the suggestion. Thus the Sisters of Charity opened houses in four major cities of Yemen such as Aden, Sanaa, Hodeida and Taiz. All these four institutions were old age homes where the poor and abandoned old people were taken care of. Most of the inmates were so weak and sickly that they had to be bathed, fed and helped out in the most basic of human needs. All the inmates were Muslims and citizens of Yemen.

In line with the agreement between the government and the Sisters of Charity, the White Fathers were assisting the Sisters of Charity till 1987. Known also as the Society of the Missionaries of Africa, this was a congregation founded in 1868 by Archbishop of Alger Cardinal Charles Lavigerie, doing very active ministry in Africa as well as in the Arabian peninsula. However in 1987 the White Fathers decided to move out of Yemen and Mother Theresa herself took interest to invite the Salesians of Don Bosco to take their place.

Accordingly, the then Bishop Giovanni Bernardo Gremoli, under whose jurisdiction the Catholic Church in Yemen falls, invited the Salesians to take the place left vacant by White Fathers. The Bangalore province of the Salesians of Don Bosco responded to the request and sent Salesian priests; Fr. Mathew Vadacherry in 1987, Fr. Jacob Kizhakkeyil in 1988 and Fr. George Puthussery in 1989 to assist the sisters and to look after the migrant Catholic population in Yemen. Of these pioneers, the first two are no more. Fr. George Puthussery, having served in the missions of Yemen for nearly 25 years is now back in Kerala, serving in a college run by the Salesians of Don Bosco at Mampetta in Calicut.

From 1987 to 2016, nineteen Salesians, including me, have served in Yemen, some for brief periods and some others for a rather long period of time.

Fr. Mathew Uzhunnalil, my own uncle about whom I mentioned in chapter one, had worked in Yemen since 1991 for a long period of 17 years. Earlier, the Economer of the province, he was 65 years old when he reached Yemen. A person full of energy and enthusiasm he managed to build a good rapport with the government and gradually managed to get back from the government two churches that had been confiscated by the government. On different occasions he had shared with me his experiences and the challenges he faced in Yemen.

Yemen was no easy mission. In fact, on July 20, 1998 there was an attack on the Missionaries of Charity Sisters working at the old age home in Hodeida. Three Sisters, Sr. Ceilia, Sr, Aletta, both from India and Sr. Michael from the Philippines were shot dead by fringe elements. After this incident the government of Yemen had put in place security forces to ensure the safety of the Sisters. Sr. Nirmala, the first successor of St. Mother Theresa, was the Mother General when this incident took place. Her composed response even in the height of sadness at the loss of three of their dear Sisters was inspiring: "Such incidents will not deter us. Our strength is in Christ Jesus. So long as these poor people would need our help we will continue our service in Yemen," she said.

Before setting off for Yemen, I had long talk with Fr. Mathew Uzhunnalil, Fr. Raju Unnaramkallel and others who were ministering in Yemen before me. They gave me valuable inputs on the possibilities and limitations of the mission entrusted to me.

All the priests who went to Yemen were allowed there on visa issued by the Social Work Department of the government and as such they were allowed to celebrate Mass only in the convents of the Sisters of Charity. How ever, through the efforts of the priests working there, and after long negotiations with the government two churches which were confiscated earlier were returned to Catholics for their worship. Besides, one of the priests was issued a religious visa that permitted Catholics to conduct public worship. This decision of the government, attained primarily through the painstaking efforts of Fr. Mathew Uzhunnalil, was a big blessing for the nearly 3000 strong Catholic population of Yemen as it provided them an opportunity to frequent the sacraments.

Many of these Catholics were Indians, several from the Philippines, some from Sri Lanka, a few from Pakistan, a few Europeans too and the rest were from other Asian and African countries. I was given a religious visa, making it my responsibility to look after the migrant Catholic population there, while spiritually assisting the Mother Teresa Sisters as well.

I reached Taiz. It took a couple of weeks for me to get into the new rhythm of work. Apart from spiritual service to the Sisters, as was my wish when I opted to go to Yemen, I got lot of free time for personal prayer; something I could only wish for during the 20 tightly packed years of work back in India since my ordination in 1990. Whenever possible in the evenings I visited families of Catholics residing there.

Although the civil war was at its initial stage only, the impact was already being felt. There were employees who were not getting salary for months, there were people who had problems with their documents; but couldn't even think of going back to their homeland as they had already

Political Map of Yemen

Bishop Paul Hinder

With the Missionaries of Charity and
Some Faithful in Yemen

By the Grace of God | 63

Welcome to Yemen

At a Eucharistic Celebration

One of the Old Age Homes
Run by the Missionaries of Charity in Yemen

invested huge amount of money to reach Yemen. There were sick people who looked forward to someone visiting them. The Sisters too used to join me on visits to houses of the faithful whenever they could spare some time from their challenging work.

The work schedule and geographical distance were difficulties for many to frequent the Sacraments. However I used to feel edified by several Catholics who used to set aside every other leisure possibilities, take a holiday from work and would turn up to make confession or to attend the Holy Eucharist. In all these cities and in the rest of Yemen, there were quite many Christians. Many of them worked in the health sector, in hospitals. There were also a significant number of people who worked in factories. The several flourishing port cities in Yemen provided employment to many in the shipping industry as well. There was a considerable number of Catholic faithful working in the different foreign embassies too.

The Sisters of Charity had four centres in Yemen. Each centre looked after around 80 inmates. The first centre to be opened was at Aden, a port city with a population of approximately 8 lakh people. Aden was the capital of People's Democratic Republic of Yemen until that country's unification with the Yemen Arab Republic in 1990. Being a big city, Aden had a number of district sub-centres. In three such centres namely Crater, the original port city, Ma'lla, the modern port and Tawahi, known as the steamer point during the colonial period, there were Catholic churches.

In Crater there used to be Mass celebrated every Friday. Since Sunday was working day in Yemen, the obligatory

Eucharist used to be on Friday evenings. Around 50 people including Sisters of Charity used to attend this Mass.

At Ma'lla the Mass used to be on Saturdays and around 20 Catholics used to gather together there for the Mass. The priest's residence was at Tawahi. Here the Mass was on Sunday in which approximately 20 people used to take part. During the other days of the week the Mass was held in the convent chapel of the Mother Teresa Sisters. The convent was nearly 18 kilometres from the church at Tawahi where the priest resided. So from Monday to Thursday the priest would take shared taxi to reach the convent for the Mass.

Sanaa was the largest and oldest city in Yemen. Incidentally, it is a world heritage city as well. According to legends, the city was founded by Shem, the son of Noah.

Hodeida was the third city where the Sisters had their institution. It is the fourth largest city in Yemen with a population of over 4 lakh people. The city with more than hundred mosques is considered to be one of the most important Islamic towns in the world.

The fourth city where the Sisters ran their centre was Taiz, a place that lies in the southwestern part of Yemen and has a population of over 6 lakh people.

Yemen was part of the Apostolic Vicariate of Arabia, operating directly under the Holy See. A significant number of the Catholics under the Vicariate were non-residents who had made this place their home for employment sake.

In January every year the priests working in this Vicariate used to come together around the Bishop to share experiences, discuss issues and get instructions. Besides this meeting, the Bishop used to make a pastoral visit to the parish during the season of Lent every year. Bishop Paul Hinder, a very cordial and fatherly person, used to carry it out without fail and always had a word of encouragement and appreciation for the priests, Sisters and faithful.

After two years of service in Taiz, I was asked to move to Aden. I was also asked by the Bishop to co-ordinate the ministry exercised by the priests in Yemen, a work that was done until then by Fr. Pudussery George who returned to India in 2012. The very next year Bishop Paul Hinder included me in his pastoral council. It obviously gave me lot of exposure to the way the Church is treading forward in the region.

Once a year, I could take a holiday and come back to India. The four of us working in Yemen used to arrange our holidays in such a way that the absence of one is made up by another. By 2014, I had already completed 4 years in Yemen. I was experiencing a lot of fulfillment from the ministry. The dedicated work being done by the Sisters was highly edifying. Sacramental ministry, visiting the sick, family ministry, time for personal prayer etc. kept me engaged all the while.

My release from the captivity of terrorists was a powerful testimony of the providence of God. I must confess that I experienced this providential care of God many times in my life even before my abduction too. One such instance that stands vivid in my memory is something that happened while I was back in India for holidays in 2014. By then my blood sugar level had already reached a stage where I was asked to take insulin twice a day.

In March 2014, I came to Kerala for holidays. Before returning to Yemen, I thought of going for a full medical checkup. This was because I realized that the instances of fluctuating sugar level and the related physical ailments were on the increase. The check up was done at Lourdes Hospital, Ernakulam. The test was done and the result ready. Of course, I expected no serious ailments except that the sugar level would be high. But there were surprises awaiting me.

There was a bad cough that was persisting for some time. I presumined that it was being caused due to some allergy. In the medical examination except for the throat my health was certified to be fine. Noticing a growth in the throat, I was asked to consult the ENT specialist of the hospital. It was one Dr. George Kuruvila. He examined the throat, checked the growth and sent the particles for biopsy. In the meantime, expecting nothing untoward, I had already booked my return ticket to Yemen. As soon as the biopsy report reached him, the doctor called me. "Father... It is a cancerous growth. You have to meet an oncologist at the earliest." It was a rather worrisome news.

"The best person to consult on the matter would be Dr. Gangadharan," Sr. Agnes suggested. Dr. Gangadharan was serving at Lakeshore Hospital in Ernakulam. But getting an appointment with him at short notice was not going to be easy. Then came a helpful intervention from my aunt who was working at Wellcare hospital in the same city. "Dr. Gangadharan visits this hospital and meets patients. He is such a wonderful person that he makes sure to meet every patient in queue, in spite of his own fatigue," she said. Thus an appointment was arranged.

I found Dr. Gangadharan to be a very compassionate person. He first examined my throat, then the biopsy report and then said. "Fr. Tom... We will do one more round of tests."

This time I was sent to Lakeshore hospital. Before the results came, I had to return to Aden. My aunt Elsamma Thomas got the report and met Dr. Gangadharan on my behalf. Doctor asked me to call him back from Aden and so I came again after a gap of thirty days or so. Doctor advised me to do one more biopsy and the intervention was done by Dr. George Kuruvila at Lourdes hospital. Possibility of throat cancer was looming in the air. It looked like I only need to know at what stage the cancerous growth is.

Although it was time for me to go back to Yemen, I was asked to wait until the second biopsy report came. Since there was a gap of a couple of days, I decided to go for a retreat, a Salesian retreat and then a second one at Attapady. The Salesian retreat was held at Don Bosco Aluva. As the usual practice during Salesian retreats I had a chat with the provincial Fr. Thomas Anchukandam. He suggested that, I return from Yemen and be the administrator of Kristu Jyoti College, the theological study centre of the Salesians, situated in Bangalore as it would help me to take care of my health condition as well. I consented to this proposal of Fr. Provincial.

After the retreat, I went to see Dr. Gangadharan with the result of the biopsy report of Lakeshore hospital. He examined the report carefully and suggested for yet another test of the same biopsy. It was indication enough for me that there was some bad news to be expected.

As the suggested test would take another two weeks, I went for attending a second retreat; this time at Attappady retreat centre. My own younger brother Joshy was assisting Fr. Xavier Khan Vattayil, the Director of the popular charismatic retreat centre Sehion at Attappadi, Palakkad in Kerala when he came to U.S. to preach retreat to the faithful there. So it was easy for me to get a seat booked, although it was last moment. I attended the retreat. It was indeed a beautiful prayer experience.

As soon as the retreat was over, I contacted the hospital for the result of the test. I was asked to meet the doctor once again.

I reached the hospital. Dr. Gangadharan smiled at me and said. "It is a borderline case. The good news is that the situation is not dangerous as yet. But you need to have a follow up. Medication and follow up means, once in six months you must keep repeating the check up of your throat." I thanked God. All those who were praying for me too were overjoyed to hear that the situation was not dangerous.

In the meantime, I was eager to get back to Yemen because the false ceiling and the roof of the main church in Aden was almost falling off and needed urgent repair. In the meantime, Fr. Provincial had already given me hints about asking me to come back to the province. He was aware of my health situation and wanted me to keep up with the check up and treatment. I wanted to finish the repair works, especially that of the roof and false ceiling, completed before I hand over the parish to the next person. His Lordship Bishop Paul Hinder told Fr. Provincial that for a newly appointed parish priest it would take months to familiarize with the systems and situation in Yemen and so the repair work would further prolong.

Fr. Provincial thus permitted my stay back in Aden to complete the repair work so that the new person taking my place would not be unnecessarily burdened. So I stayed back in Aden and got fully immersed in the repair works of the church. In the month of May 2014, my new assignment as administrator of KJC arrived. However Bishop Paul requested Fr. Provincial for an extension of my stay by a few more months as the works were still in progress.

By then my replacement, Fr. Antony Panikkarukunnel was trying to get his papers ready. He reached Sanaa the capital of Yemen in the month of November 2014. He worked in Hodeida parish for about a month. In August 2014, I came back for a checkup of my throat at Lourdes Hospital, Ernakulam where, the doctor after the examination told me that, everything was ok and I need to have my chest check up after an year. The joy was doubled as I could bless the wedding of my nephew Vince Augustine, the son of my elder brother Augustine, who had passed away in an accident on the 21 November, 1988, when I was doing my third year of theology.

I returned to Aden to resume the supervision of the renovation of the church. Hardly a month later, I got the bad news over the phone from my elder sister Mary that our beloved mother passed away to the Lord. I made the trip to Ramapuram on September 8, 2014 for the funeral of my mother and I returned to Aden. The repair works were all over by December 2014, and his Lordship Paul Hinder arrived in Aden and blessed the renovated St. Francis of Assisi Cathedral church at Tawahi, Aden and installed Fr. Antony Panikkarukunnel as the new parish priest of Aden. I stayed with him for a couple of weeks to introduce him to the work and the people around who are known to us. In February 2015 although my visa was still valid, I was already back in Bangalore province.

My assignment this time was to be administrator of Kristu Jyothi College, a centre for theological studies. Since it was already the fag end of the academic year, I did not officially take charge as administrator, but started helping out Fr. Gilbert who was handling the additional workload of administration along with the teaching of theology. Even as I reached KJC, Bangalore, in February 2015, I was having a return ticket for Aden and a re-entry visa valid for three months. I was to return to Aden by 24 April 2015 and surrender my visa and put another priest in my visa position.

In a way, it was nice to be back at KJC, the place where I had spent four years of my life; doing my theological studies from 1986 to 1990. I was in the company of my own former professors, companions and around 100 energetic seminarians pursuing their theological studies. The academic year at Kristu Jyoti College ended on 19th March. There were some summer programmes, repair and maintenance work of the building etc. that kept me busy for weeks even after the academic year concluded.

It was
indeed a
pathetic
situation for
the people
with no
electricity,
water and
the basic
necessities
of life.

POLITICAL TURMOIL IN YEMEN

Chapter 5

By the time I left Aden, the law and order situation in Yemen had deteriorated beyond all control. To understand the reasons for this dangerously failing law and order situation, one needs to understand a bit more about the modern political history of Yemen leading up to the present conflict.

Yemen is one of the oldest centres of civilization in the Near East. At the start of the 20th century, North Yemen was under the Ottoman Empire while Southern part of Yemen was under the control of the British. North Yemen became independent at the end of World War I in November 1918 and became a republic with the overthrow of the theocratic Imamate in 1962.

South Yemen became independent from Great Britain on November 30, 1967. In 1970 the new South Yemeni nation became the only Communist nation in the Arab or Muslim world, and naturally became an ally of the old Communist Soviet Union. This put South Yemen at odds with the more tradition-minded North Yemen, and made enemies of the pro-Western and conservative neighboring nations like Saudi Arabia.

As with many other countries in the world, the two Yemens were dragged into the Cold War rivalry between the United States and the Soviet Union. The North and South Yemens went to war against each other in 1972 and 1979. In 1978 Ali Abdullah Saleh became president of North Yemen.

In the late 1980s, the two Yemens discussed the possibility of peaceful unification, and in May 1990, the two nations merged into one Republic of Yemen. Four years later, tensions between the conservative North, which dominated the new nation, and the more progressive South erupted into a short but bloody civil war. South Yemen declared independence, but lost the war.

Most Yemenis are of the Sunni sect of Islam. However there is a large religious minority belonging to the Shiite branch of Islam who live in the North. The tensions between these two prominent groups made matters worse as Shiites accused the Sunni branch of joining hands with Saudi Arabia and annihilating them while the Sunnis accused the Shiites of creating trouble by joining hands with Iran. The Houthi rebellion began in 2004 by Hussein Badreddin al-Houthi, head of the Shii'a Zaidiyyah sect. Tensions between Yemeni security forces and the Houthis first flared up when the group's supporters protested in mosques in the capital, which the then-President Ali Abdullah Saleh saw as a challenge to his rule.

Saleh ordered the arrest of some group members, and urged their then-leader, Hussein al-Houthi, to stop the protesters from disturbing the worshippers. The first war began when President Ali Abdullah Saleh sent some troops to the province of Saada to arrest Hussein Badreddin al-Houthi, who refused to curb his supporters. Hussein al-Houthi was killed in 2004 after Saleh sent government forces into Saada. The years-long intermittent war ended in a ceasefire agreement in 2010.

The brief calm was prelude to the storm in store. In 2011, the Arab Spring spread to Yemen. Demonstrators, including many Houthis, filled the streets of Sanaa and other cities, demanding the resignation of Ali Abdullah Saleh, who ruled the country with the support of Yemen's most powerful tribe. When the tribe joined the protesters in the streets, Saleh was forced to resign in February 2012 and his vice president, Abdrabbuh Mansour Hadi, was installed as his successor.

Hadi inherited a weak and divided security apparatus and was never able to assert control over the fragmented country. A National Dialogue Conference created a new constitution and set up a six-region federal system, but the Houthis declared they were unhappy with the deal and vowed to resume their rebellion also wanting to have more share in the ruling of the country.

In the meantime, Saleh continued to meddle in Yemeni politics, undermining President Hadi by making alliances with his political enemies and retaining the loyalty of nearly two third of the country's security forces. When the Houthis began advancing from the north, the ousted strongman saw

War-torn Yemen

War-torn Yemen

War-torn Yemen

War-torn Yemen

War-torn Yemen

With the Lord, With the Flock

that an alliance with his former mortal enemies could pave his way back to power.

In September 2014, Houthi fighters swept into the capital Sanaa and forced Hadi to negotiate a 'unity government' with other political factions. The rebels continued to apply pressure on the weakened government, until after his presidential palace and private residence came under attack from the militant group, Hadi resigned along with his ministers in January 2015. The following month, the Houthis declared themselves in control of the government, dissolving Parliament and installing an interim Revolutionary Committee led by Mohammed Ali al-Houthi, a cousin of Houthi leader Abdul-Malik al-Houthi. However, Hadi escaped to Aden, where he declared that he remained Yemen's legitimate president, proclaimed Aden as country's temporary capital, and called on loyal government officials and members of the military to rally around him. When Houthis took over Aden, Hadi escaped from Aden to Saudi Arabia's capital Riyadh and sought assistance. Accepting the request, Saudi Arabia formed a coalition of Arab states and began bombing the Shiite Houthi rebels on 26th March, 2015.

There was every possibility of a full-fledged war. Taking note of the precariousness of situation, India's Ministry of External Affairs (MEA) issued advisories as early as January 21, 2015 to Indian expatriates in Yemen to leave the country. Two days before the attack by the Arab coalition, the MEA issued an urgent advisory urging all Indian citizens to evacuate as soon as possible. However, more than 5000 Indian citizens had not heeded the warnings and were trapped in Yemen.

In this context, the Ministry of External Affairs along with the Indian armed forces ventured into a daring humanitarian operation to evacuate the Indian citizens trapped in Yemen.

As Yemen was not accessible due to a no-fly zone, India chose Djibouti as a centre for initial evacuation by sea. Indians in Yemen were advised to reach Sanaa and Aden. The Indian Navy redeployed the patrol vessel INS *Sumitra* to the Yemeni port of Aden. Besides the government made provisions for protection and support to Indian ships and aircraft in the conflict zone. The Indian Air Force deployed two C-17 Globemaster cargo aircraft with a capacity of 600 passengers to Djibouti.

Two ferries belonging to the Lakshadweep administration, MV *Kavaratti* and MV *Corals*, with a capacity of 1,500 passengers were dispatched to Aden. In addition, two Airbus A320 aircraft of Air India were also deployed to Muscat in neighboring Oman.

On 1 April 2015, INS *Sumitra* reached Aden to evacuate 349 Indians. When Air India was permitted to fly to Yemen on 3 April 2015, it started evacuating people from Sana'a to Djibouti and Djibouti to Mumbai or Kochi. On 4 April 2015, INS *Mumbai* reached Aden but was unable to dock due to shelling, so the people were ferried to the ship in small boats.

Over the days more than 4,640 overseas Indians were evacuated along with 960 foreign nationals of more than 41 countries. Out of a total of 5,600 people, 2,900 Indians were evacuated by 18 special flights from Sanaa and 1,670 Indians by Indian Navy ships from four ports. The air evacuation ended on 9 April 2015, while the sea evacuation ended on 11 April 2015.

For more than three months a fierce battle raged between the Saudi-led coalition troops and the rebels in Aden. It was indeed a pathetic situation for the people with no electricity, water and the basic necessities of life. People suffered greatly without food, drinking water and other basic necessities of life. Hospitals were overflowing with the injured due to bombing and fighting. Slowly, the rebels were pushed out from the city of Aden by the coalition forces and anti-Houthi forces and finally the city was cleared of the rebels.

He went
to the car
and brought
out all the
four Sisters
and lined
them up.
Their hands
were still
fastened.

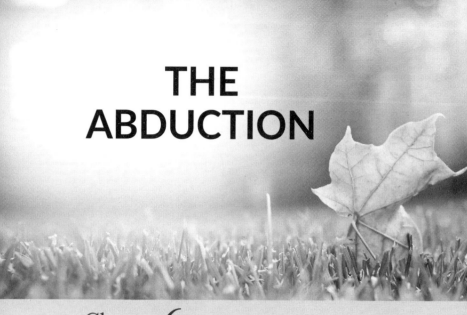

THE ABDUCTION

Chapter 6

In the first week of April 2015, I made a visit to Don Bosco Provincial house in Bangalore which is hardly 10 kilometres from Kristu Jyoti College, where I was serving as administrator. April 5 was Easter Sunday and I wanted to greet Fr. Provincial and talk to him as I had been away from the province for some time. In fact, Fr. Thomas Anchukandam, the provincial, who gave me the appointment to go to Yemen had completed his term by January 2015 and the new provincial Fr. Joyce Thonikuzhiyil had already taken charge.

I met Fr. Joyce, the provincial, in the office. A very good listener, he intently heard all I said. I told him that my visa, unlike that of the three Fathers who were evacuated from Yemen, is a religious visa. The other Fathers, as I mentioned earlier, were working there on a visa issued by the social work department of the government and so had no direct responsibility over parishes.

"Being the only religious visa holder priest in Yemen, I feel obliged to be there with the suffering faithful who are entrusted to my care," I told Fr. Provincial. "I am willing to go back to Aden provided someone else is put in my position as administrator in KJC," I continued.

"But haven't the faithful mostly gone back?" asked Fr. Provincial.

"Very many have gone back. But there are many still hanging on, hoping that the situation will slowly improve. Besides, there are some for whom moving out is impossible for various reasons," I said, as I was still in touch with several who were still holding on there.

Fr. Provincial again asked me, "Have you told your brothers and sisters, won't they have any objections?"

I answered, "My parents are no more. I don't foresee any objection from my brothers and sisters except perhaps my immediate elder sister Mary".

Fr. Provincial kept thinking. He obviously seemed worried about my safety.

"There are two more reasons why I feel obliged to go," I added.

"Some of the workers and caretakers in our centres are still there. They cannot go back to their countries until they are relieved and their accounts settled. If no one does, it they will have to leave and go back to their home countries empty handed. Knowing them and their families, I feel it my responsibility to intervene."

The discussion went on for some time after which he gave me consent. I knelt in front of the Provincial and requested him to bless me. He prayed over me and gave me the blessing of Mary Help of Christians.

Since my visa was still valid, I could set off for Yemen in two week's time. However, due to the war-like situation in Yemen, I couldn't directly reach Yemen. I went to Abu Dhabi first and met Bishop Paul Hinder and took his blessings. Arrangements were made to go from there to Djibouti via Nairobi. Bishop Georgio received me at Djibouti airport and took me to the Bishop's house.

Djibouti diocese is a small one with only a handful of priests. Bishop Georgio Bertin, Fr. Mark, Fr. Tom Donavan, Fr. Eder, Fr. Jean Bertin, and Brother Solomon Ponraj (from Tamil Nadu, now a priest in the diocese), and another brother. There are four or five parishes or mission centers some of which I visited and celebrated the Holy Mass.

There I waited for more than a month as I could not cross over to Aden. By the second day of my arrival in Djibouti, there was a ship leaving for Aden port but as some of the permissions were lacking, I could not go by that ship. Perhaps, God did not want me to go by that ship for I learned two days later that, there was an air bombing in Aden port on the following day of the arrival of that ship causing large-scale destruction.

Mr. Henok, the Ethiopian youngster, who had earlier stayed with me in Tawahi, Aden, used to send me whatsapp messages and pictures of the bombing, people dead on the streets, the attack on churches etc. He was still staying on in Aden in our church residence, taking care of the church and property of St. Francis of Assisi church at Tawahi, Aden. He risked his life many a time. The Lord Jesus protected him from all harm! He was there in the Sisters' home when I would later reach Aden on 1st July, 2015.

On 21 May 2015, I completed 25 years of priesthood. To celebrate the occasion there was a Eucharistic celebration in the Cathedral church in Djibouti followed by a dinner. The day was made memorable by the presence of several priests, Sisters and the faithful of Djibouti. I spent the month visiting the mission centers and repairing of some electronic and electrical equipments at the Bishop's house.

While in Djibouti in the third week of May 2015, I had a dream in which my father Varghese, mother Thresiakutty and my elder sister Mary were standing beside me. My father was showing me a nodding gesture with the head, indicating a permission being given. No one spoke. I woke up in a short time. Is that nodding a signal from heaven for me to move on to Yemen? Perhaps yes !

Fr. Tom Donavan drove me to the airport to see me off to Sanaa, Yemen. Before leaving for the airport, on the previous day, I had my confession made to him, the next one only in Rome in September 2017.

Thus after a month-long wait, on 2 June 2015 I managed to reach Sanaa by a UN Red Cross flight which was carrying medical supplies to Yemen. I was the sole passenger in the flight. At Sanaa I was received by Fr. M. K. George sdb and the five MC Sisters. There I had to wait patiently again for one month.

Now I could see for myself the toll that war took on the beautiful country of Yemen. All key places including airports were bombed during the war. Most of the bridges were destroyed too, making transportation very difficult and dangerous. The law and order situation had crumbled. With no effective monitoring system in place, the fringe elements were taking law into their hands. Long curfews, shortage of provisions, not even hospitals having enough personnel or stock of medicines to cater to patients made life miserable for the people. Travelling by road, one could be intercepted, abducted, shot at or looted anywhere on the way. Power supply, communication system, water supply etc. in most places were either partially or fully dysfunctional.

At the end of June 2015, I had received permit to travel by road to Aden, which was rather dangerous, considering the law and order situation. I had to cover a distance of nearly 450 kilometres by road with most streets witnessing frequent open firings and bombings.

I decided to move to Taiz which was 180 kilometers before Aden and waited for the best opportunity to move from there to Aden. Then war was at its peak at Taiz as well. The rebels had set up camps on the mountainous side of Taiz while the government led forces were attacking them from the air, down the mountains. Our church building stood right in the middle of the crossfire. Sound of bullet shots, explosions, noise of airplanes booming in the air, military trucks speeding on the roads, sound of ambulances rushing with the wounded were all routine events for weeks.

While in Taiz one afternoon there was a shootout and showers of bullets hit the Sisters' house on the first floor room, breaking windows and piercing through the linen the Sisters had put out for drying. Providentially, all the Sisters were in the ground floor and none of them got injured.

As soon as the situation calmed a bit, on 1st July 2015 I moved over to Aden. The driver of the MC Sisters at Taiz drove me to the taxi stand and arranged with a taxi driver there to reach me safely to the Sisters' home in Aden. Thus I reached Aden.

The Church area in Aden was already destroyed in the bombings. The Sisters' house was at a distance of 18 kilomters, and travel up and down from the church residence at Tawahi to the Sisters' home was almost impossible and unsafe. My option now was to stay in a room in the campus of the old age home run by the Mother Teresa Sisters. This room was adjacent to the convent chapel and very close to the old age home and the residence of the Sisters, all in the same big campus.

The Sisters, the few Christians who remained on and the other acquaintances were extremely happy to see me. They narrated to me their own face off with death during the days of bombing. Once the war started, many migrants went back to their home countries. Countries including India evacuated their citizens. But not all could do so; leave everything and go. Some remained on for some time hoping the situation would improve, but eventually had to escape. However there were many who couldn't really escape to anywhere. Some had made Yemen their home for various reasons. Some others had invested practically all their wealth there and so moving out meant starting all over again from scratch. Some people couldn't afford a risky journey with sick and bed ridden people at home.

Once the war started life became very risky. The price of provisions shot up. The long hours of curfew meant that people couldn't come out to buy even the essential commodities they needed. With the law and order situation out of hand, instances of looting and robbing increased steeply. Public utility services such as banks, telephone, water supply, electricity, telecasting, town-cleaning were all interrupted either partially or fully due to the war.

The people who remained on there told me several incidents of narrow and miraculous escapes. I could see marks left by gun shots on the walls of most buildings around. In many places there were huge heaps of debris left after bombings.

Amidst stories of loss, tension, fear and tragedy there were some silver linings too. I remember Sr. Sally, the superior of the convent sharing with me about how they experienced the providence of God during the days when the war was at its peak. The Sisters had nearly 80 inmates to be looked after. Foreseeing the war they had stocked enough medicine. But couldn't do the same with regard to food, as preserving several food items was rather impossible in the given circumstances. At one time the Sisters reached a point where their stock of food practically ran out. 'We can skip the food if needed. But we cannot leave the inmates hungry. Many of them are sick and under medication,' Sr. Sally told her community members. There was no point in going out to purchase provisions as shops were not open. Most of them had run short of provisions or wouldn't open their shutters for fear of being looted. They served the supper for all the patients that evening but did not know what they would serve the next morning. Sisters started praying intensely.

Early in the morning, a stranger took permission from the security persons and came in to meet Sr. Sally. He was a Muslim from the neighborhood. "Even ordinary families with few members are running short of food," he said. From somewhere he brought enough bread for all the inmates for the next day. He did not stop at that. This continued for the next two weeks. Then one day as he came with the bread he told Sr. Sally. "Now it has become almost impossible to get bread from anywhere. I won't be able to bring you bread anymore. But I can help you in another way. I will get you few sacks of wheat powder. You can use it for food. Let us hope that before that too gets over the situation will return to normal." True to his word, the man brought few sacks of wheat flour the next day. Sr. Sally told me that this God -sent help enabled them feed the inmates during the most turbulent days of the war.

Back in Aden, I tried to get in touch with the flock that was still remaining on, besides meeting up with other people I knew around there. But it was no easy task. Whomever I met had some tragic incidents to narrate. They were all just hoping that the crisis would soon be over.

The Sisters too were immensely happy that I was back. They were unable to have the Sacraments for months due to lack of availability of priests. This was true of the Catholics who remained back as well. Besides the daily Mass we used to individually and as a group spend long time in prayer imploring the intervention of the Almighty to normalize the situation in the country. Since moving out for any pastoral ministry was impossible, I spent a lot of time in prayer in the convent chapel. Now living in the same campus, I used to visit the inmates in their wards. They too were under a lot of stress due to the war situation. The Sisters were doing a very edifying job of looking after them. Many of them had to be bathed and fed as they were terminally ill. After the prayers in the chapel, the Sisters used to begin the day, giving bath to the patients, cleaning them, dressing them up etc. Only after all these, would they even have their breakfast.

The institution had nearly 100 inmates, including the workers and caretakers. I found that there were quiet many things that lay in wait for repair as they couldn't find technicians to repair things during those days of war. The technician in me awoke. I spent a lot of time everyday trying to repair fans, electricity connections, coats, chairs, taps, pipes and the like. The ITI experience of course came very handy for me in doing this.

There were five Sisters in the convent. Sr. Sally the superior was from Kalayanthani, near Thodupuzha in Kerala, India. Then, there was Sr. Ansalem another Indian Sister from Orissa. There were two Sisters from Rwanda. Sr. Margret who had been in Yemen for several years and one more Sister, Sr. Judith, in the community. Sr. Reginet who incidentally was the youngest of the group, was a temporarily professed and was waiting to go to Amman to make her perpetual profession. Unfortunately, the war-situation had prevented her from travelling out of Aden and joining her companions to make the perpetual profession. In fact, Sr. Sally, the superior had sent one of the security men to Sanaa to bring her passport to Aden so that she could be sent as and when a flight from Aden to Jordan would be available. This security man was on his way back to Aden on 4 March 2016, when the attack took place.

Every ten days or so, I contacted Fr. George M.K who was at Sanaa, Hodeida and Taiz in turn. He too was battling heavy odds, risking everything to see that those entrusted to him were taken care of. One day Fr. M.K called me to inform that he was fleeing Taiz. He asked me not to make any telephone calls to his number until he called back. When safe, he would call me back was the understanding. I spent that entire night in prayer in my room in Aden.

Life went on this way for some time. The rebels were pushed out of the city. But normalcy did not really return. The political atmosphere continued to be one of tension and uncertainty. The night the rebels were evicted from Tawahi, Aden port area, the church of St. Francis of Assissi there, was attacked. I made a visit to the church at Tawahi and felt very sad, seeing the church severely vandalized.

The Christmas of 2015 was celebrated on 24th evening with the five Sisters and to be precise with seven other faithful. I don't want to mention their names for their safety as they are still in Aden. After Mass we had the Santa Claus distributing gifts and dancing. We did not know then, that this was the last Christmas for the four dear Sisters, Margaret, Anselm, Judith and Reginet. Thanks to those seven faithful who made the difference that day ! May Jesus bless them and strengthen them in their faith.

I had requested the Sisters for a special Christmas gift, a plastic barrel of 250 liters capacity. And they gave me that in gift wrapping. I spent the next weeks trying to work out a bio-waste gas production unit. The experiment was partially successful as the gas began to come, but not combustible. Modifications were being made as I continued with experiment.

"In the morning on Friday, 4 March, 2016, after the Eucharistic adoration followed by breakfast, I was praying in the chapel. Friday being a public holiday, the Mass was scheduled for the evening to facilitate the participation of some Catholics around the area. However, little did we know of the shocking incidents which would unfold that day.

After my prayers in the chapel of the Sisters, I went to the kitchen, greeted Sister Judith who was preparing the midday meal for the five Sisters and me. I did not know then that I was greeting her for the last time. I checked the gas plant from the window, to see if the drum that collects the gas was up or not. I came out of the house and took a walk around the house where plants were being watered. I shifted the water hose to another tree and came to the front side of the house. The gardener, an Ethiopian, Mohammad by name, came to the front area of the Sisters' house. I showed in signs that I shifted the water pipe. All the same, he went to the back of the house to see it for himself. Hardly 10 feet away was the gate leading to the Mother Teresa Home campus. I took three or four steps forward and there I heard the gunshot and a shooting sound from near the main gate which was around 30 feet from the place where I was at that moment. Of course, a compound wall separated my view of the main gate. Another four or five steps, I was out of the small gate and entered the

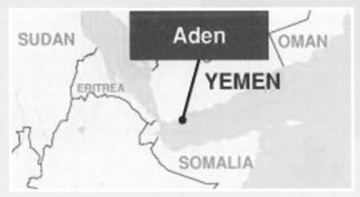

Aden

A Church Building in Aden Destroyed by Bombing

The Blood of Martyrs

Reign of Terror

Martyrs for Christ

In Captivity

main campus. Soon a man carrying an automatic gun, with a chain of bullets on his shoulder, and face covered, took hold of my hand. He was in Yemeni soldier uniform.

"I am an Indian" I said. I was not panicky. But as I glanced around, I understood the seriousness of the situation. I was told to sit in the chair that was outside the security room. In the meanwhile, the gardener came running out of the Sisters' home compound, and was going towards the place where the switch for the water pump was positioned. He was shot from the back on his left side. He fell dead instantly on the drive. Since he was not wearing any shirt, I could see the blood gushing out forming a pool on the drive. The one who shot was having a silencer automatic gun, so much so, no sound was heard, except just as much as a hand clap.

From what I guess, the attackers must have been four or five in number. I saw three of them in the compound. As their faces were covered it was impossible to identify any further details of them.

While sitting on the chair they noticed my mobile phone, a small one, in my shirt pocket. The man guarding me and the gate asked for it and I gave it to him. Just then, out from the security room came the son of the cook of the old age home, a boy of ten or twelve years; all shaken. He was told to sit beside me on another chair. In the meanwhile, a third person searched the rooms beside the main gate where the worker boys stay and brought out one who did not go to the Home for work that day because he was not feeling well. He was brought to the security room and was shot there. I could only hear the muffled sound of the gun and the emptied shell of the bullet fall out from the door.

I have no idea, how many were there in that room breathing their last. Then they opened the main gate and drove in a car and parked it in the drive on the left side of the gate, on my left side. The gate was closed and the man carrying the silencer gun walked across the drive to the old age home. He entered in and after a little while brought two Sisters, Anselm and Margret with hands bound with plastic fastener, placed them in the car and went the same way again back to the home. Just then Sr. Judith who was cooking in the Sisters' home, with a plastic bucket in hand entered the drive to the home, to join the others in the morning duties of caring for the aged. She was obviously unaware that two Sisters with their hands bound were already in the car. I don't think she saw the bleeding men on the drive.

In a short while, there came Sisters Judith and Reginet with hands bound. They were placed in the car; now four of them. I have no idea what was going on in their minds at that time. Just then, the bleeding man lifted himself on his hands, asking for some water to drink. The boy beside me said to the man guarding, that the bleeding man was asking for water. The reply seems to have been 'do not worry about him'. In the meantime, the one who brought the Sisters out, went in a third time and came back to the main gate. This time no one was with him. I didn't hear any gunshot now. But I presumed he must have finished off the fifth one, Sr. Sally in the home itself.

I did not know what went on in the home for the aged. How many were killed there? He went to the car and brought out all the four Sisters and lined them up. Their hands were still fastened. By now they must have prepared themselves to go to the eternal home. No crying, all silent, like sheep being led to the slaughter house. Then he made two Sisters, Judith and Reginet walk the drive towards the home and then to the right side into the garden. Now, I could not see them anymore. They were on the other side blocked by the compound wall of the Sisters' home. Shortly, I heard two gunshots. Then the man came back to the other two Sisters, made Sr. Margaret to walk to the left side of the drive. She was shot at point blank on the head from behind. As I heard the sound, I saw her fall forward face down. Then Sr. Anselm was moved a little forward on the main drive side and on the left in the garden. The same procedure was followed. I heard the last gunshot and Sr. Anselm fell forward with her face to the ground. While I heard these four gunshots I prayed in my heart, 'Lord have mercy, Lord have mercy, both on the Sisters and on their killers.'

Next would be my turn, I guessed. I said a prayer in preparation for death in my mind. "Jesus Mary and Joseph... I give you my heart and my soul; Jesus Mary and Joseph, assist me in my last agony; Jesus, Mary and Joseph; may I breathe forth my soul in peace with you".

The man who asked me to sit on the chair came forward and said; "Go to the car". I stood up and went to the car. There was no point in resisting. If it is for martyrdom I was ready. Perhaps, their intention is to shoot me and then drive off, I thought.

As I reached near the vehicle the one with the silencer gun asked me, "Muslim?" I said; "No...I am a Christian." Then he said something which means a 'non believer'. I was confused a bit. What they did now, was contrary to what I expected. I was thinking they would finish me off there. He made a telephone call to somebody and spoke in Arabic. Then they opened the boot of the car and asked me to get inside.

He helped me get into the boot. It was rather spacious and he pushed on my head from top to get me fit into the space. He lifted my legs and put them in the boot. I was not blind-folded nor were my hands and feet bound. Someone closed the boot. It was all darkness inside. Now, I thought, they would take me out of the compound and kill me somewhere else. After a few moments, the boot was opened again. Someone threw a bundle, white and violet clothes into the boot of the vehicle. As it was dropped in, I heard a metallic sound. The boot was closed again. In the darkness, I tried to feel the bundle that they threw in. To me it felt like the altar cloth and altar cover from the chapel. Since it made the metallic sound, I thought it to be the Tabernacle wrapped in the altar linen and the pink altar cover of the Lenten season. 'Yes...It is the altar cloth,' I whispered to myself. I could not make any effort to open it to verify, for it fell near my feet and I had no space to move and check. 'The Eucharistic Lord is with me,' I thought to myself and prayed.

> **It brings tears into my eyes when I think of the merciful protection of the Lord that kept me going for such a long period of time without any medicine.**

LIFE IN CONFINEMENT

Chapter 7

Is the Lord accompanying me on this journey of uncertainty? I kept praying. I was pretty sure as to how many consecrated hosts were there in the tabernacle. Hardly a month after my arrival in Aden, I had noticed that the tabernacle was not fixed tight enough. So I had told Sr. Superior that it should be fixed. This is why I thought it must be the tabernacle. Later when I was freed and was able to speak to Sr. Sally over the phone from Rome, after my first press meet in Rome, I came to know from her that she had got it fixed the very next day, and that the tabernacle was there in the chapel itself, which she was able to go to the chapel and verify after the attackers had gone off with me as captive.

The cook's son told her that they took me away in the boot of the car. She did not see the sacred species. The ciborium was with water and no hosts. She thought that

I got alerted and consumed the hosts. As the crucifix was lying in the place where I normally sit to pray, in a thrown position and my breviary thrown there, she thought I was probably hit with the crucifix on my head.

By then the vehicle started moving. After driving for nearly 15 minutes or so it stopped. Someone opened the boot and helped me to come out. I was asked to get in quickly into another vehicle where they blindfolded me. I was no longer able to see. They drove for some more time, then the vehicle came to a halt.

Someone held on my hand and led me forward. From the feel of the atmosphere around I thought they are leading me into a house or building or something. I could feel some doors through which I passed as I was being led forward.

"Do not worry, you are in safe hands." At this point someone reassured me. They made me sit in the room on the floor, against a wall, on a sponge-like material. Later they served me I believe, lunch and water to drink. Now I was blindfolded; but hands and legs were not bound. Later, I asked permission to go to the toilet. They led me by hand to the bathroom and untied the cloth with which they had blindfolded me. When I came out, they again blindfolded me and led me to the same place to sit there.

Why am I here? I asked myself. The mission the Lord had given me was to be present to the Sisters till their very last moment. We were praying together to the Lord for the end of war, for conversion of ISIS and Al-Qaeda and for peace in Yemen all these months. Now that the holy Sisters have been martyred and I am not killed, God must be wanting me to pray for my captors sitting in their own dens.

In the evening they asked me to hand over all the personal belongings still left with me; my wrist watch, the pen in my shirt pocket, a small pocket booklet on which I used to jot down things, my rosary and the set of three keys, one of my room, one of the Sisters' house, one of the main gate and a comb were handed over. My spectacles and foot wear had already fallen off at the time of getting into the boot of the car. They asked me to strip myself and change into the clothes they provided me with. They took away the steel chain that was on my neck, looked at the medals on it and said, 'Miriam.' I said 'yes' for they were medals of Mother Mary and of Don Bosco.

Then they tied my hands and feet with clothes. Still blindfolded, I was made to sit on the soft material on the floor against a wall. I could lean on the wall. There was some Arabic music going on loudly. What went on from the morning kept on flashing in my mind. Surrendering myself to God's will, I prayed for strength to fulfill the mission He has for me in my life.

I could feel the presence of an air conditioner in the room. I was not allowed to sleep. I sat on the rather soft thin mat on the floor. When your eyes are shut your other senses rise to the occasion and try to assist you better. The ears help you pick up noises around that you never heard when your eyes were wide open. Your nose starts giving you clues about your surroundings. All on a sudden I heard the footsteps of someone coming in.

I felt the presence of a person in front of me; "Eat", the person told me as he kept the plate in my hands. My right hand reached out to the plate in hand. It felt like some kind of a biriyani rice with a curry mixed in it. I could not see what I was eating. Thoughts flashed through my mind as to how blind people could be relishing their food without seeing what they were eating, except through their smell, taste and touch. I was learning to perform different acts without the sense of sight. The person must have been watching the way I was trying to manage the situation. He served some drinking water in what felt like a bottle. He also allowed me to wash my hands with water and took away my plate when I was done with my meal.

After my meal, I rested for some time. Later I expressed my need to attend to nature's call. One person led me by hand to the toilet and at the door my blindfolding was removed. When I was done, the person once again blindfolded me and led me back to the mat.

Footsteps again! Someone pulled out my blindfold once again. Now I see three people in the room. One of them has a camera in hand. As on earlier occasion, the faces of all of them were covered with the head-gear-cloth except for their eyes. The man facing me told me something in Arabic. I did not understand what he said. However, seeing camera in the hands of the man who gave me the instruction, and the accompanying gestures I more or less deciphered his request as 'look on to the camera'. Two of them held something behind me like a backdrop to the photograph. I could not turn back to see, what exactly was it, that they were holding. They took some photos of me.

Once they were done with the photographs, they tied my hands and legs once again with a cloth. The knot was obviously tight. However, the length of the cloth provided some possibility for me to move my hands and legs within the tied position. I could lie down, but it was difficult to get up, as my hands were tied behind. This was causing rather severe ache on the shoulders too. I realized that I should keep turning on my side, otherwise my hand and shoulder muscles might go numb and thereafter I may not be able to turn at all. However, on the second or third day, someone apparently noticed my discomfort, untied my hands and loosely tied them in front. The consideration was on condition that I should not try to open my blindfolding. I agreed and in my heart thanked the Lord Jesus for this concession. Now I could rest on my back and get some sleep.

Day or night made little difference to me. Perhaps it was on the second day that a person who spoke some English asked me for information as to my native place and the cities I visited in India. He asked me whether I had travelled to other foreign countries, what I was doing in Yemen, names of people I know in Yemen etc. Then he asked for the telephone numbers of those whom I know; those of my brothers, sisters etc. In all honesty I said that I did not really remember any telephone numbers except the landline number of my mother. I told him that my mother was no more, and so, that telephone connection was not operational anymore.

Life went on uneventfully for a few days; The same routine.

A couple of days later, they walked in, this time with a video camera. One of them handed over to me a piece of paper on which there were written a few sentences in English.

"We want you to face the camera and read that text." One of them told me in broken English. It was a handheld camera. One of them brought a chair from outside and made me sit on it. The content of the statement I was asked to speak was a request to the Pope, the Bishop and the government of India to intervene for my release. I saw 8 March 2015 as the date mentioned in the statement and thus presumed that 4 days had now passed since I was taken captive. There was no point in resisting. I spoke in front of the camera, what they wanted me to speak. The video recording was over and the group left the room. Life was back to the normal routine.

After a week and a half or so, (I can only make a rough estimate as I had no way of keeping track of date, day or time), I heard the sound of some new voices. They were discussing something in Arabic. The next day, I believe they shifted me to another place. I was blindfolded and made to lie down in the vehicle. It might have been an ambulance. I was dressed in a burqa. From what felt like a thin tube fixed on to my hand on the one end, perhaps they were trying to make me look like a patient being rushed for medical care. The vehicle must have run for approximately two to three hours.

After some distance they shifted me to a car. Now I could hear the voices of women and children in the vehicle. We must have been moving out of the city of Aden for I could feel the change of weather. On reaching the destination, I was told not to make any noise nor try to run away. It must have been a mountainous area of Yemen at a higher altitude. The climate was cooler here. It seemed to be a residential area because I could feebly hear the murmur of children from the neighbourhood; may be from the same house where I was now. The prayer calls from a nearby mosque also made me feel that I was not in a lonely area and that there were people around. I could also hear the sound of heavy vehicles at a distance. Occasionally I could hear sound of heavy gunfire; at some other times sound of airplanes too.

They kept me in a room on the ground floor for one or two days. It must have been a big hall, for I had to walk some distance to reach the toilet. A few days later they shifted me to a room on the first floor I believe, because I had to walk up some steps; may be ten or fifteen to reach the new room. The new room was obviously smaller than the first. The distance to the toilet was much less, but not within the room. The routines remained just the same here as well.

Someone would bring the food on time. I would eat it in silence, wash the plate and keep back the plate on one corner of the room. My nails had already grown really long. Left with nothing to trim them, I used my own other hand to break off the edges of my nail. Although there was no mirror in the room, I could feel that my beard and hair were growing wild. I was allowed to take bath only once a week. One day through gestures I asked the man who brought the food for a nail-cutter. He seemed to have understood my sign language. It was given on the same day. On another day I asked for something to apply on my hair as it had become very dry and shampoo was provided. The dress that I was given when I reached there had become very dirty and so one day I asked for a change of clothes which arrived after a day. The new set, a long garb looked pretty much the same in style as the old one. It was a huge relief for me as I could now wash the clothes that I had been wearing for some time. I washed it and spread it in the room itself for drying.

Then one day, once again three people walked into the room with a camera in hand. I was asked to sit and was given the lines that I had to say. However, what was different this time was, they pretended to beat me, trying to create an impression that I was being tortured. But I must admit that they did not inflict any physical pain and were just simulating before the camera; I presume their intention was to exert pressure on those trying for my release. This must have happened in the month of April or May 2016.

Once I had fever and I asked for a paracetamol tablet. They gave me one tablet almost immediately. By the grace of God I believe, the fever did not persist and I was well the next day.

Probably well into the month of May 2016, one morning, the place experienced an earthquake. There was some commotion. All of a sudden I heard the loud cry of children. I too felt the tremor. In fact, due to the tremor I was moved from the place where I was lying down. Some people rushed into my room to see if I was okay. "Do not get frightened", someone shouted. I could clearly hear the loud clanking of windows, doors and vessels. The tremor lasted three to four seconds. I prayed in a low voice: "Jesus... Save us all." Mild tremors were experienced a few hours later also.

It is in this place that I asked for a sign from the Lord. I asked the Lord in prayer if all the Sisters who were killed in Aden are enjoying heavenly bliss. The Lord was gracious enough to give the sign that I prayed for. A few days later I asked for a similar sign if I would be set free and this time too God heard my prayer and gave me a sign. But when I asked for a sign again if I would be set free that month itself I failed to get an answer. 'I should not put my Lord to the test', I thought to myself. From then on I started praying for the grace to fulfill His will in my life in Yemen as well as during the rest of my life here on earth.

In this place in the toilet room, the tap water was flowing very feebly only. Probably, the tap required a cleaning. Wanting to set it right, I asked for a thin screw driver. They provided me with one. With it I was able to open the tap and clear the block. We could now get the bucket filled quickly. They expressed happiness about this work, for possibly they all were using the same bathing room. Thanks to the Lord Jesus for all these moments of happiness even when I was in captivity. Here they used to give me warm tea on cold evenings. Sometimes even special noodles, somewhat like the maggi noodles we get in India.

I might have stayed in that place for almost four months. Then, they shifted me to another place, which again meant a three or four hour long, blindfolded journey by vehicle with a stopover in between.

The room at the third place had an attached wash room. The climate seemed to be similar to that of the previous place. Here again I was kept blindfolded initially. But it was rather loosely tied. Even in this place, I was down with fever for a day. As earlier, with the tablets that they gave me, I recuperated quickly. One person used to give me food and warm water to drink. An extra blanket was also given to me, as it was very chill there during nights.

One day I learned from one of my captors that Sr. Sally, the Superior, whom until that moment I thought was killed, had narrowly escaped the attack of 4 March, 2016. I was very happy to hear that. I thanked God for protecting her and for saving her life.

After a period of time, they shifted me yet again to a fourth place.

This time the journey was much longer. When we began the journey, I was in my usual clothes, given by them. How ever, during the drive I was asked to wear the burqa, probably because we had to pass a police check post. Two other people who were taking me to the place also wore the burqa to give an impression to the police that we were women. Some other people, one or two adults and children were brought in a car and we all travelled together. After sometime, the people who had joined us alighted and we continued the journey. The journey to the fourth place did not take place at a stretch, but with breaks of one or two days in between. At this fourth place there must have been five or six persons, all apparently new. There were one or two individuals in the group who could speak English. The room where I was kept must have been about 12 feet by 10 feet and with good ventilation and sufficient lighting. My stay here must have been from sometime towards the end of July or August 2016 to September 2017 until my release.

Just like in the third place, they were serving me food and drink. The place was much quieter and appeared to be a mountainous region because the climate was cool here as well. Here, they gave me two blankets which was a huge relief. They also allowed me to look at the sunlight through the window.

Once they brought a doctor and he did a check-up. After the medical examination for blood pressure and blood sugar, they perhaps realized that my sugar level was very high. I asked them the sugar level reading. They told me 'it is 450'. They asked me for the name of the insulin I was taking and the tablets for diabetes. They gave me insulin for one or two days, but told me a couple of days later that the names of the tablets I told them were unavailable in the locality.

Possibly due to the unavailability of insulin, they gave me a packet of tablets. It was a packet of 30 metformin of 1000 mg which was insufficient for 30 days. This must have been in the month of December 2016. A few days later, a photo was taken with the date note 27/12/2016 written on a piece of paper, which I was asked to hold in my hand. This meant Christmas was just two days earlier! During the next few weeks, I tried to spiritually live the spirit of Christmas in my heart. After a gap of just one or two weeks when I finished the 30 tablets they got me another 100 tablets of metformin. This time it was of 500 mg. I took one tablet in the morning and one in the night. It went on for 50 days. When it was over again there came a gap of two weeks without medicine after which they brought me another packet of 100 metformin tablets. Now I took only one tablet at noon. So it lasted for 100 days. This supply got over two weeks prior to my actual release.

Since 2014, I had been taking insulin every morning and evening. The very fact that I was protected for 557 days without any major illness is nothing short of a miracle. Except for these tablets mentioned above, it brings tears into my eyes when I think of the merciful protection of the Lord that kept me going for such a long period of time without any medicine.

The only reading material I ever got was the leaflet on the medicine packet. It was in English and the font very small. Whenever there was bright light in the room, I went through the instructions and learned about the working of metformin in the body and the possible side effects of it.

In the first month of my stay in the fourth place of captivity, I felt one of the senior guards showing me extra kindness. He used to move out once in a way and when he returned, he would bring something special for me. Sometimes he brought chocolate bars, sometimes oranges or apples or even bananas. His extra care and concern puzzled me. However I thanked God for the kindness this man thought of bestowing on me. I used to pray for all of them that Jesus would give them the grace to grow in the goodness that I experienced in them.

One day this man who was kind to me whispered into my ears. "If you want I shall quietly set you free in the night when everyone is asleep." In my heart I suspected it to be a test for me. Perhaps, they wanted to know if I would attempt to run away when I get an opportunity. I replied loud enough saying: "I do not want to run away, in that way, even if you are going to kill me." One good thing they did here was to allow me to move around the room and do some exercises. After being kept tied down for months, I certainly enjoyed moving around within the four walls of the room, stretching myself a bit.

All this while, from 8.30 am on 4th March 2016, to the moment of release no fear of death overtook me. I was not crying or trembling. The Lord gave me the courage and the grace to remain calm in my mind and heart. Many thoughts of my past life came to my mind, my failures and short comings. I asked pardon from the Lord. I had received the Sacrament of Reconciliation eight months ago, in May 2015, while waiting in Djibouti. I offered my agony in reparation for my sins and short comings. I promised the Lord in prayer that I would receive the sacrament of reconciliation at the very next opportunity.

One day, something made me pray that God should give a rain as sign from heaven that the Sisters are now enjoying the Beatific vision. Believe it or not; that evening there was a very heavy shower.

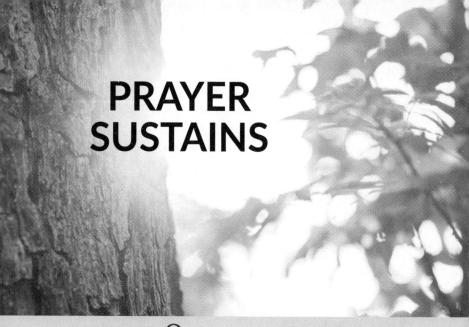

PRAYER SUSTAINS

Chapter 8

My abduction, I believe, was transformed by my life of prayer. The spiritual formation I received in my family and in my congregation definitely strengthened me to face this ordeal in the right spirit. I was brought up in a pious Christian family where daily prayers were attended by all. We said our daily rosary without fail. We had frequent Scripture reading at home. Later, as I grew up, I went frequently for Mass. I also had the singular privilege of attending the funeral of Blessed Kunjachan. I saw many touching the holy person's mortal remains, especially with sacred objects. I did not do anything of that sort. However, I prayed fervently to be gifted with the zeal that the saint possessed, as I touched his hands and kissed them.

In the congregation, I was regular enough for my practices of piety. There were no extraordinary efforts to pray. But, I must say that I was pretty comfortable with the ordinary.

I was definitely devoted to our Blessed Mother. I must confess that occasionally I missed praying the Rosary, but not my love for the Blessed Virgin. I was faithful to the celebration of the Holy Eucharist. I must have rarely missed it, largely due to sickness.

When the unforgettable day of abduction finally dawned, I found myself totally disposed. We, the community of Sisters and I, were prepared for this day. Two weeks earlier, in a casual conversation, Sister Sally, the Superior, had spoken boldly about the beauty of being martyrs for Christ. She was speaking about the gift of dying together for Christ. "I am not afraid to die", I told her, "If this is what the Lord wants, then I am ready for it."

"When in captivity, in the shadow of death, did you at any point of time regret that your return to Yemen was a misadventure"? This is a question that many, including media persons asked me after I was released. My answer is a clear 'NO'. I left India in the month of April 2015 for Yemen for the last time. But, I could enter Yemen only in the month of June. From the day I landed in Yemen, there was not a single day of regret, not even a moment. I came to do the will of God.

At this point, I must add that as a professed religious, once we get the blessings of our superiors, we need to just fearlessly cast our nets into deep waters. Before I left India, I remember vividly kneeling down before my Provincial Superior and seeking his blessings. I did that with deep faith. The Blessing assured me, "I am with you, till the end of time" (Mt 28:20). The words of our Lord, "Do not fear those who kill the body but cannot kill the soul; rather fear him who can destroy both soul and body in hell" (Mt. 10:28), were constantly in my mind and heart. The danger of death was very much there in the air. As I was thinking of martyrdom, I also wanted to prepare myself for it. Since Fr. M. K. George was the nearest priest available to me, I thought I could at least make my confession to him over the phone. But, that never materialised because of the unique war-situation at that time.

I must make clear that the call to be a missionary did not take root in me all of a sudden. It was always there in my formation days in the seminary. I frequently requested my Provincial Superior to send me to the North Eastern missions in India or to Africa, but that request was not granted as there was a greater need to render service in my province.

As I was being taken captive, I saw the Sisters fall by bullets. I prayed in my heart, "Lord, forgive them, for they know not what they are doing" (Lk 23:34). At this critical moment, I was all the more resolved to offer my life. I was taken to different places. I never knew where exactly I was. Initially, I had a bit of struggle to adjust to the inconveniences, but later on, the abductors themselves provided me with some facilities that could help me to live with minimum comforts.

I must admit that the period of abduction was not one of severe deprivation. I was offered the facilities that could help me to cope up with life. I could pray my Rosary. I prayed for all my relatives, the confreres of my province and my friends. I remembered many by name. Those whose name I could not remember, I prayed for them too.

I Prayed for the Holy Father. I remembered the deceased confreres of my province. I also prayed regularly for my Provincial Superior and the Bishop of Abu Dhabi, as I presumed that they must be really going through anxious moments due to my abduction. I was aware that many of these people might be suffering a great deal because of my captivity. I prayed for all the people, whoever came to my mind. I was praying God that they may be consoled in these moments of trial. By God's grace, I had memorized all the prayers of the Eucharist. I could thus celebrate the Eucharist without any difficulty. Obviously, I did not have with me all the things essential for the Eucharist, but, I believe God knows all.

I prayed for my abductors too. I prayed that God may bless them with a change of heart. At times, they taunted me by ridiculing the Holy Trinity. I often repeated, Lord, forgive them. I did not have much conversation with them. From my room, sometimes I saw them praying the *namaz*. As and when they prostrated during their prayer moments, I extended my hands with the intention of blessing them and praying God that better sense may prevail on them.

One fine day, they came to my room and told me that they wanted to make a video. All that I had to do was to obey orders. I did it without resistance lest the situation worsen. Although I felt extremely difficult to speak derogatively of the Holy Father, ecclesiastical authorities and some of the leaders of my country, I had no choice otherwise. I could never wish that in order to protect myself, I could permit myself to speak disrespectfully of these esteemed persons. I now sincerely seek pardon from these individuals. I must reiterate at this juncture that I was prepared to die and I told the Lord to take me away if it was His will.

During my days of captivity, I used to pray the Angelus, the Divine Mercy Chaplet, the Holy Rosary and I used to pray also for the dead too. I often thought of the Sisters who were martyred. I thought that they were privileged to be martyrs. I questioned as to why the Lord did not want me to embrace martyrdom. But, as always, I believe that the Lord has His own plan. Initially, I thought that all the Sisters were martyred, but later on I learned from the abductors themselves that only 4 of them were killed, and one of them escaped their cruelty. I knew for sure it is Sr. Sally, as I had seen the other four Sisters, two of them fall by the bullets and the other two being led to a corner of the building at gunpoint.

It happened on a day, perhaps seven months, since my captivity. I was in the third place of confinement. One of the captors, one who speak to me in broken English, showed my profile picture in his mobile phone and said 'you look nice in the picture.' I asked as to where he got this picture and he said, 'Downloaded from Google.' Then he asked this question; 'Are not these women afraid of life?' I thought to myself that he must be referring to the Sisters: So my reply was, 'why? All the five Sisters are dead.' Then he said, 'No, only four were killed, one escaped through the fridge.' The Arabic word for fridge or flask is 'Thaloja.' This word I learned while being in this place, because, he provided hot water for me to drink in a thermo flask. And it was called, 'Thaloja.' I thanked God for preserving at least one of the Sisters.

The heroic, yet tragic, martyrdom of the Sisters kept disturbing me a lot as I lay in captivity. In the community, when I lived with them, there was a lot of fraternity among us. They were literally angels for the inmates of the institution. In my disturbed mind I kept asking God if the Sisters were already with Him in heaven. I kept pleading with God for a tangible sign that they are in His company in heaven. In fact this was the biggest preoccupation of my prayer in the initial days in captivity.

One day, something made me pray that God should give a rain as sign from heaven that the Sisters are now enjoying the Beatific Vision. Believe it or not; that evening there was a very heavy shower; there was lightning and thunder as well. Looking at the rain through the window and feeling the lightning and thunder I thanked the Lord in my heart. The Lord has heard my prayers. Given the situation in which I was, He could not have given a clearer sign. The pain I was feeling within at the martyrdom of the Sisters vanished at that point. In fact, I started praying to them as well to intercede for me that I too may, like them, remain faithful, brave and steadfast in faith.

I do count this event as an extraordinary one. By hindsight, I see how the Lord accompanied me throughout.

During my seminary days, I loved the hymn "One day at a time, Sweet Jesus, that's all I am asking from you..." It was a hymn written by Marijohn Wilkin and Kris Kristofferson in 1974. It was composed by Marilyn Sellars. We never realize how the hymns that we sing when we are young, inspire us later on in our lives. They come so handy especially in our moments of difficulties. I could hum this song repeatedly and that made a great difference in my dark moments.

Now, I wonder how I lived through eighteen months of my detention. How did I manage? I really never felt despair during these moments. I lived one day at a time. Thus, I never felt that it was unbearable. The Lord was helping me moment by moment. It was all in His plan. I knew for sure that the prayers of several were backing me up. After my release, I learned that several thousands of people across the world prayed and made sacrifices for my sake. Among the innumerable people, there were also brethren of other religions incessantly praying for me. No wonder, I felt fearless in facing the unknown.

I am particularly enamoured by the condition of my health. I was given some medication and also a visit from a doctor to check my blood pressure and blood sugar.

I remembered the passage from the Gospel according to Mathew, "Are not two sparrows sold for a penny? Yet not one of them will fall to the ground apart from your Father. And even the hairs of your head are all counted. So do not be afraid; you are of more value than many sparrows" (Mt 10: 29-31). I felt very precious in God's sight. The Lord was making use of me. And, the prayer of St. Francis of Assisi, "Lord, make me an instrument of your peace..." was some thing that was constantly coming to my mind and heart. I wanted to remain as his instrument. "Let Him do what He wants," was my heartfelt prayer.

Once the words of the Gospel take deep root in us, we can be sure that no amount of terror can shake us. The

Word of God becomes alive and it is no mere text. The incarnation becomes real. I felt the close presence of God in these moments. During the Eucharists that I celebrated there, the words of the Gospel were coming not from my head, but they were like a fountain flowing from my heart. The words were real for me.

Whenever I thought of the Sisters who were shot dead, I prayed, "Lord, have mercy on them, on the Sisters and the killers." I do not know why I am still alive. Why the nuns and the inmates were brutally murdered and I was absolutely unharmed. I have no clue whatever. I consider it God's special grace that I am alive. Each one of us has a mission to accomplish. I have a mission and that is to serve the Lord till the end, even at the cost of my life. I did not preach the Gospel to them, as the ambience wasn't favourable. I only prayed for them. The abductors prayed faithfully five times a day.

It must have been two or three weeks before my actual release; one fine morning I began to experience very severe pain on my left shoulder for no reason. I could not lift my left arm above my elbow. I asked the Lord in prayer 'why Lord?' then I lifted my left hand, supported by the right and held it stretched and prayed, 'How much pain you will have suffered when you hung on the Cross on three nails: receive this pain of mine for my own sins and that of others.' I held the hand in that position for a little while and then put it down. In two days time all my pains disappeared without any medication. Thanks to the Lord Jesus !

Whatever happens, happens according to the plan of God. We need to just offer ourselves to God. The words of

Jesus, "But even though, because of my name, you will be hated by everyone, not a hair of your head will perish" (Lk 21:17-18), appeals to me now more than ever before. No harm can come to us without the Father's knowledge. He is such a providential Father. How true are the words of Jesus! The Heavenly Father is so good and He has preserved me from death. This only implies that He has a purpose for me. Thus, I am ready to serve Him anytime, anywhere.

My ordination motto was exactly the same, "I have come to serve and not to be served" (Mt 20:28).

Get up...
Change your
clothes.
Be quick.
We got to go.

BACK TO FREEDOM

Chapter 9

Footsteps at this hour?

It is still dawn. My captors usually visit me at later hours of the day. This is too unusual. Of course, from the time of my captivity, everything has been unpredictable. Why are they here? Am I being shifted yet again to another location?

The last few months of my stay in this place had been very much untroubled. My captors ensured medical assistance. While in the previous two places I had been blindfolded whenever the captors visited me, here I just needed to cover my face with a cloth. Perhaps, the captors trust me. Certainly, they know that I would not run away.

Captors trusting the captive? Unusual though.

"I bring you good news. We are going to send you home to Kerala. Have a bath quickly and change your clothes." Did I hear it right? Incredible! One can't be sure till the last episode of the whole event! Yeah, but at this hour? Unusual!

It is now approximately more than a hundred and twenty days since the last video was taken or shot. The video was shot on April 15, 2017 (going by the date on the cardboard sign that was placed on my lap while shooting the video). Since then, I have consumed a hundred and ten diabetes pills. So at least four months have elapsed. This then should be the first or second week of September.

It should be less than three weeks that I began asking the Lord, "What next?" In fact, I had been contemplating about the many brave martyrs of the Church all across the centuries from all over the world. The words of Tertullian, 'The blood of the martyrs is the seed of Christianity' became meaningful to me ever since I witnessed the cold-blooded murder of the MC Sisters on the day I was taken captive. They were given the privilege of bearing witness to the Lord by becoming martyrs. In the last few weeks, I had prepared myself to embrace martyrdom if the Lord found me worthy of it.

But now I hear my captors calling out, "we are going to send you home to Kerala". I had been contemplating about and awaiting my eternal home! *"May His will be done."*

I went immediately for my toilet needs and rushed to get dressed with the clothes that they provided: the one in which I came out in Muscat, the capital of Oman. They brought a burqa and put over my clothing. 'Hurry, board the vehicle quickly,' said the man. I did that and we started off. The journey was through a bumpy path. I could not see the path nor the surroundings. By noon or so the vehicle reached a good road; no more shake up. The vehicle halted and waited for nearly an hour. In the meanwhile, I could hear them make some phone calls, all in Arabic, which I could not follow. A little later someone declared; "The arrangements are not ok. We have to return, to the place where we were staying." The car started its return journey through the bumpy path. Just before we reached back one of them told me:

"You must have been praying to the Third Person of your God; now begin praying to the Second Person the rest of the day and night, so that, arrangements will be ok by morning. Keep your clothes without soiling."

All our liturgical prayers end with the words, 'Through Christ our Lord,' calling on the second person of the Holy Trinity. I praised God, for in their words I am reminded that all prayers made to the Father through Jesus is answered. *"May His will be done"*.

Just at the time when the sun recedes into the horizon, the vehicle makes a halt. We have reached back. I am accompanied back to my room. I removed the burqa. Inside the room I do not have to wear it.

I am back inside the four walls of my confinement. These four walls are silent witnesses to the story of my life in the last few months. In spite of being confined physically to these four walls, I have never lost my freedom. My body is confined,but my spirit wafts in freedom. Who could ever take away my freedom to pray; my freedom to speak with my Lord in the silence of my heart; my freedom to be lost in

Back to Freedom

Thank You, Sultanate of Oman

God Answers our Prayers

With Pope Francis

With the Salesian Community at Vatican

With the Apostolic Nuncio and others in New Delhi

contemplating eschatologcal realities? It is precisely because of the freedom to pray that I have remained serene, calm, unperturbed, composed ever since I was confined to a room.

However unusual it may seem, I am unperturbed by the events of the day save the excruciating backache because of the rough and bumpy road travel of the day. Pain prevents sleep. This pain can be vicarious. What better way to accept pain than by offering it to the Lord together with the Blessed Mother praying the Rosary contemplating the sorrowful mysteries?

I had my food and laid down to give rest to my back. I had a nap too. Back pain subsided. It must have been the middle of the night, footsteps were heard again. Again the instruction: "Get up ... Change your clothes. Be quick. We got to go."

Again?

I obey. Do I have a choice? Religious life has taught me to be obedient. But in religious life, there is scope of dialogue. While in circumstances such as this, there is no space for dialogue. It is dark. And yet the burqa has to go over my face. This time there are two of them accompanying me to the vehicle. The same bumpy road? *"May His will be done."*

The journey begins. After some hours the vehicle halted and in a short time I was shifted to another car and the journey resumed. The warm rays of the sun, piercing through the clouds and through the burqa over my face, gently brought me to realize that we had reached the place where we waited the day before at noon. But this time however, we are not alone; we are accompanied by another vehicle. Who could be in the other vehicle? Are they those who were supposed to have come yesterday to free me from my captors? What delayed their arrival? Their delay led to another to and fro travel along the bumpy and rough roads.

"Breakfast is ready"! The train of my thoughts is derailed. The captors had thought about providing me food for the journey; breakfast in the car - after a very long time.

It is unbelievably surprising to realize that my captors have so much of goodness also in them. Till this moment, they had been treating me well taking good care to provide me meals on time, providing medicines for diabetes. Never did they hurt me physically or verbally. Torture? an absolute 'No'. But it was this same group of captors who mercilessly shot the Sisters and others in *Missionaries of Charity Home* in Aden.

Perhaps, they were brainwashed into such erroneous ideologies. Goodness and evil emanating from the same individuals at different circumstances! What to make out of it-innocence being exploited by fundamentalists for their wicked agenda?

As I travel through these very disturbing thoughts, the vehicle has travelled into a sandy desert. The other vehicle that brought us breakfast followed us all along. A sudden gush of gentle breeze and an equally gentle tap on my weak shoulder woke me up. The drive is now very smooth. Perhaps, we are on a tarred road. Perhaps, there are trees along the road.

My captors are no ordinary men. They are very meticulous in planning to the smallest detail of everything they do. While I was wondering why the other vehicle was accompanying us for almost three to four hours with just a driver in it, both vehicles pulled over for a while. One vehicle moved off and I was served lunch. Then we waited in the car till about 3.30 or 4. 00 pm.

I hear another vehicle approaching us and halting. Someone opens the door of the car and holding my hand, leads me to the new vehicle. There the face cover over me is lifted. It is the driver of the vehicle that came just now. In his mobile, he browses through the photo gallery. Selecting a photo in the mobile, he matches the face in the photo with the face of the frail and weak person sitting in front of him. All of a sudden the atmosphere around me changes dramatically. The driver smiles signaling that the two faces match and asked me, 'is this you?' There are two others in that car. But dead silence.

"Don't worry. You are in safe hands". After a very long time a sentence in perfect English. God, assuring me through the words over the telephone handed to me by the driver. Everyone who interacted with me from the moment I was taken captive spoke in Arabic or in English that was so broken that I could barely understand what they meant. This assurance put some kind of an end to the great uncertainty I was feeling from the moment we started off from the room. May be God is assuring me through these people. Mysterious are His ways. I have experienced this assurance right from the moment when I was captured. Since then, together with the psalmist I have prayed, "Keep me safe Lord" (Ps 140:4). "You are in safe hands", is God's reply. The Sisters at *Missionaries of Charity Home* were martyred - The *Safe Hands* kept me safe. I was shifted from one location to another - The *Safe Hands* kept me safe. I was confined to a rather dark room where I lived, having lost the count of days- His *hands* kept me safe.

The driver takes the wheel. We are back into the desert roads. This time, we are accompanied by two other vehicles. Two vehicles full of fuel for the journey? We may have to travel a long distance. The whole dramatic travel beginning from yesterday has exhausted and worn me out. How long is it going to take?

Around dusk, the driver decides to stop the vehicles. I am allowed to remove the purdah over my face. We are in a desert hemmed in by the blue sky littered with bright twinkling stars. I gather from the conversation of the drivers that we are in the desert of Saudi Arabia. Our vehicle is refueled. Meanwhile, we dine on our frugal menu in silence listening to the music of the dusty wind. We move on at a speed of 180 km/hour, through the desert.

"Welcome to Oman!" said the driver. It must have been about 3.30 am on 12th September. The other vehicles that accompanied us disappeared. We entered a tarred road and drove for about half an hour or so. We reach a camp - border camp. There is disciplined silence in the camp - fruit of rigorous training to discipline perhaps. My burqa is removed and I disembark from the car.

Someone walks towards me. He starts checking me up

the way a doctor would. I guess he is a doctor. There is some interaction still. Possibly he has reported that I am fit to travel further. I am escorted to a helicopter that is by now gathering momentum to fly free out of the circle. The driver accompanies me into the cabin. In just a few minutes I see an aerodrome. As we alight, I see three people waiting for us. One among them, in broken English enquired about my health. Detailed planning and comprehensive arrangement for my release.

"You will be taken to Muscat, the Capital of Oman"; announces the doctor after a brief medical investigation and leads me into the flight. No security check. Disciplined silence inside the cabin. No sign of curiosity about the passenger. No eyebrows raised. Indifference? Ignorance? Rehearsed? But I am the only passenger. Even the attendant serving me snacks maintains sacred silence. Unusual indeed!

Breaking this continuum of silence, I am informed that *His Majesty Sultan Qaboos bin Said*, Sultan of Oman had secured my release. God's ways are indecipherable and incomprehensible. He has used people I have only heard about, to secure my release.

"The Press will be waiting for your declaration. Prepare yourself. We are about to land." An instruction was given in chaste English by one of those who joined me in the flight.

I am filled with sentiments of gratitude to the Lord and to all my dear brothers and sisters praying all over the world for my release. How must I briefly verbalise my thoughts?

We alight.

Instantly my thoughts turn to God the Almighty, the Safe Hands for preserving me to this moment. "I thank God Almighty and Oman's Sultan Qabood bin Said for securing my release. I also thank my brothers and sisters and all relatives and friends who were praying for me". Silence! Press declaration over.

We move quickly to a posh hotel. Detailed arrangement again - a doctor; new sets of clothing; a pair of shoes and shaving kit and perfumes.

I look into the mirror. Is that me? No, it is so unlike the 'me' that I had seen in the mirror before I was captured. I am bearded and disheveled. I have lost weight. After a shave that took real long time, a refreshing shower followed by food, I meet the doctor. The weighing machine showed 56.5 kilograms as my weight. A brief medical chat and we are off to the airport again.

I am told that now I am in the cabin of the flight taking me to Rome. The doctor in the cabin administers intravenous medication. I flew to Yemen with the mission to offer spiritual assistance to the Sisters of the Missionaries of Charity. Now, I fly from Muscat! My mission now may be to witness to the truth that the Lord God is, one who hears and answers our prayers.

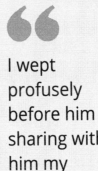

I wept
profusely
before him
sharing with
him my
experience.
He was so
sympathetic,
compassionate
and
concerned.

IN GRATITUDE

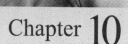

Chapter 10

"Wake up! We are flying above Rome! Get ready! We are about to land!" - one of the aircraft crew woke me up as I was asleep due to the sedation given a few hours earlier.

Suddenly I realized that I was aboard a plane and not on the 'bare floor' of my little 'room' which I was so accustomed to, for several months. How many months? Honestly, at that moment, I could not recall exactly how many months I was under the custody of the terrorists! I wondered whether it was just a dream, or I was really going to breathe the air of Rome. I was told by someone: "Today is Tuesday, 12th September, 2017." I had absolutely no idea of the time, the day and the month!

At the Ciampino Airport in Rome where I landed around 5 pm, accompanied by a few officials who had flown to Oman to receive me and take me to Rome, I was quickly taken to an official vehicle and driven to the Salesian community inside the Vatican State, there to be entrusted to the waiting Salesian community – Don Sergio Pellini, the Rector and four other members of the community, including Fr. Abraham Kavalakkat who in the days that followed was to accompany me during my visits and to the various meetings. Along with the Salesian community of the Vatican were present three Salesians from the Generalate, Rev. Fr. Francesco Cereda, the Vicar of the Rector Major, who on behalf of the Rector Major had been following up my case throughout the period of my captivity, Fr. Saimy Ezhanikatt, his secretary and Fr. Thomas Anchukandam, who during his term as Provincial had first sent me to Yemen and who presently is the Director of the Institute of Salesian History, Rome.

I was received with great warmth by this representative group of my confreres with the traditional Indian shawl and flowers. I was extremely glad to see Fr. Thomas Anchukandam there – my Professor and former Provincial.

I was truly happy, because I had reached where I belong!

I expressed my desire to celebrate Holy Mass for the first time after the 3rd of March 2016. I made my confession and celebrated thanksgiving Holy Eucharist.

The most-memorable event was yet to take place–the meeting with Pope Francis, the Holy Father. It was on Wednesday morning after the regular General Audience. I found myself standing before the Holy Father at his Santa Marta residence. I couldn't believe my eyes! I was deeply moved. Cardinal Oswald Gracias, Archbishop of Bombay, and Fr. Abraham Kavalakkat accompanied me.

I knelt down and kissed the feet of Pope Francis. Immediately, the Pope responded by helping me up and embracing me. Then came the most surprising moment! The Holy Father kissed my hands! He kissed my hands twice! The Pope is the representative of Christ. I bowed before him. He held me in his arms. Usually we kiss the hand of the Pope, but in my case, it was he who kissed mine. What a humbling experience.

I wept profusely before him sharing with him my experience. He was so sympathetic, compassionate and concerned. I cannot expect anything more than this, I have been given a new life and I requested the Holy Father to thank all the people for the prayers offered for me all over the world. At that moment, I remember saying these words to the Holy Father: "In captivity I prayed for you every day, offering my suffering for your mission and for the good of the Church."

I saw the Pope with tears in his eyes! He then blessed me. I continued: "Truly, every day, I felt Jesus close to me. I always knew and felt in my heart that I was never alone." The Pope whispered to me that he prayed for me.

Meeting the Holy Father was a great grace bestowed on me because of my captivity. I also had an audience with Pope Emeritus Benedict XVI. He too said he prayed for me.

Later, I re-lived those moments when I saw the same in pictures published by the Vatican newspaper *L'Osservatore Romano*.

On the same day, that is, Wednesday, 13th September, at 6 pm. I called my cousin Navitha Elizabeth Jose. I could feel her great surprise and joy when she heard my voice. In fact, it was Fr. Abraham Kavalakkat who spoke to her first. She told me that my phone call to her will remain as the most precious memory in her life. I told her to convey my thanks to the people, relatives, church heads and politicians. She was constantly in touch with the Salesian priests, Church leadership and others along with all the members of my family. I told her that I was quite alright and that my medical check-ups were being arranged. Fr. Abraham told Navitha that my return to India would be decided only after I regained full health. In fact, I was advised to remain in a Salesian community in Rome for a few days before heading to my homeland.

The Honourable Minister for External Affairs of India, Mrs. Sushma Swaraj called me over the telephone expressing happiness over my safe release. She wished me speedy recovery and reassured all helps from the Prime Minister, the government of India and from her own person. The cardinals and archbishops in India too called over the phone to express their happiness and assured the continued prayer accompaniment of the church in India.

On Saturday, 16th September, at 10 am there was a press conference organized by the ANS – *Agenzia Notizie Salesiane* (Salesian News Agency), at our Generalate. When I reached there I was received by H.E. Reenat Sandhu, the Honourable Indian Ambassador to Italy and some other representatives of the Indian Government, Fr. Francesco Cereda, the Vicar of the Rector Major, Fr. Guillermo Basañes, the General Councillor for the Missions and a number of other confreres. The Rector Major too met me immediately before the Press

Conference and told me how proud he was of me and how relieved he was to see me personally at the Generalate. Later the Rector Major would put around my neck the Missionary Cross which he was wearing himself telling me that the cross represented the members of the entire Salesian family, who were accompanying me with their loving and sacrificing prayers for my safe release.

During the press conference itself, I was flanked by Fr. Ángel Fernández Artime, the Rector Major, and Fr. Ivo Coelho, the General Councillor for Formation, an Indian. Fr. Ivo acted as interpreter for me. The Press Conference lasted about an hour.

"I thank God Almighty, He has been extremely kind to me. No gun was pointed at me. He kept me healthy enough." I told them that I hoped to get a new passport soon, after which I could return to India. I was not juggling with any serious health issues. I had only lost weight due to diabetes and not starvation. At the memory of the Sisters and helpers who were killed on that fateful day of 4th March 2016 in Aden, I couldn't control my emotions. My voice quivered when I publicly expressed my condolences. "I thank God Almighty for this day. He has kept me healthy enough, clear in mind and emotions under control until now."

When one of the journalists asked me whether I was harmed physically by my captors, I had no hesitation in telling him: "I was never physically harmed during captivity. I thank God Almighty, for He has been extremely kind to me. No gun was ever pointed at me. He preserved me healthy enough."

Answering the query of one of the journalists, Fr. Ángel Artime Fernandez, the Rector Major, replied: "No one ever told us that they asked for money. No one asked us for even a Euro. We don't know anything about this. This is the whole truth. And I believe that Father Tom knows even less."

The journalists, as usual, were curious to know more about my one-and-a-half years spent in captivity.

"In captivity I had enough freedom, within limits of course. My captors asked me how old I was and when I answered to it as 58, they told me "Don't worry, you will live up to 85". I celebrated two birthdays (August 18) in captivity.

"I never felt threatened by the terrorists. They moved me to different locations blindfolded. Yet they did not harass me in any way, and cared for me when I fell ill. I believe that the prayers and sacrifices of so many people made them treat me well."

"I could get up and walk around as I pleased, and they even asked me to exercise to feel better. They never threatened me in any way."

"Since I had plenty of time at my disposal, I prayed and exercised my mind by celebrating the Holy Mass in spirit and in truth."

At the Press Conference, I was particularly touched by the presence of about 30 Sisters and Brothers of Charity, founded by Mother Theresa. I was truly overwhelmed by emotions during my brief meeting with them immediately after the Press Conference.

Later, on Tuesday, 26th September, Mr. Jomy Thomas, a reporter of the *Malayala Manorama* Newspaper who had flown all the way from New Delhi, had a personal interview with me. He asked me how I stayed strong through the ordeal even as I saw the people around me gunned down? This is what I told him: "As the Lord lives, not one hair... will fall to the ground..., that assurance of Jesus stayed with me. That fortified me. I was not afraid."

To the question whether I would go on another assignment, I had no hesitation in saying: "Of course, if God wills so. I will even go to Yemen, if it is God's will for me. I have no fear of death. My only desire is to carry out God's plan for me. I leave it in the hands of my superiors to guide me in fulfilling God's plan for the rest of my life."

"Will you forgive your captors as an individual?" the reporter asked, a pertinent question.

"I can only answer that question as a priest. Christ has taught us to love our enemies. It was natural for me to forgive them. I have been praying for them from day one."

Fr. Harris Pakkam sdb, of the Vatican Salesian community, interviewed me for *The New Leader*. He asked me about my general feeling about the whole episode that I had gone through during the last 18 months. I told him: "I am happy that I have gone through this experience and it has made me strong in every sense, and now my heart goes out in gratitude to God for this new life He has given me. I cannot thank Him enough for the miracle that he has done for me."

I flew out of Fiumicino Airport on the evening of 27th September. My two-week stay with the Salesian community at the Vatican proved to be an ideal setting for my recovery, as it helped me to get the necessary daily medical attention, kept me protected from unwanted attention at a time when I had to recoup my energies and provided me with the possibility of meeting some selected confreres and ecclesiastical dignitaries, notably, His Lordship, Msgr.Paul Hinder, Vicar Apostolic of Southern Arabia, with jurisdiction over also Yemen and Msgr. Stephen Chirappanath, the Apostolic Visitor for the Syro-Malabar faithful living in Europe as well as some other representatives of the Kerala Church. I also had an opportunity to visit the Pontifical Salesian University and address the confreres. On Tuesday, 26th September, I was once again at the Generalate to greet and thank the Rector Major and his Vicar, and to give my final message to the Salesian Family. I am grateful to the Rector and all the members of the community, especially Frs. Abraham Kavalakatt and Harris Pakkam for their very personal concern for me during my stay with them.

I remember with gratitude the doctors of Vatican hospital who took care of me. They took pains to thoroughly examine my physical and psychological health and administered all the needed tests and medication. The chief doctor Mr. Pontecorvi co-ordinated the task. In the first couple of days once every two hours the doctors visited me and monitored my health situation. They are responsible for my speedy recovery and return to India on 27 September, 2017. May the Lord Jesus bless them and their dear ones for what they have been to me.

After a rather long journey with lots of experiences to think about, at 7.10 am on Thursday, 28thSeptember, I landed at the Indira Gandhi International Airport, New Delhi. During the journey from Rome to New Delhi I was accompanied by Fr. Freddie Pereira, and Fr. Mathew George, the secretaries of the Provinces of Bangalore and Kolkata respectively, as well as an official from the Indian Embassy in Italy.

It was indeed a home-coming.

I was received by Mr. Alphonse Kannamthanam, the honourable Minister of State for Tourism, MPs Mr. Jose K. Mani and Mr. K.C. Venugopal, and several political leaders from Kerala. Archbishop Kuriakose Bharanikulangara, the Archbishop of Faridabad, Fr. Joyce Thonikuzhiyil, the Provincial of Bangalore, Fr. Jose Koyickal, the Vice-Provincial of Bangalore, Fr. Jose Mathew, the Provincial of New Delhi, Fr. Albert Johnson, former Provincial of Trichy and Fr. M.K. George, who was with me in Yemen, were also there to receive me. I was so happy to meet my Provincial and the Salesian confreres whom I missed for a long time as well as my family members! My eldest brother, U. V. Mathew, who is 72, and my elder sister, Mary, were almost in tears as they saw me near the exit gate. There were present also several priests and nuns, especially a host of Salesian priests from the nearby communities. I could see how difficult it was for the security personnel to control the media persons, as dozens of journalists jostled for photos and videos as I was led outside through the VIP gate of the Indira Gandhi International Airport. As it was obvious, people around me were asking several questions. I was really overwhelmed to see the number of people who came to the airport, all of whom had been praying for my release.

Someone asked me about the demands made by the captors, and my reply was this: "Initially they asked who'll

With the Rector Major Fr. Artime Àngel Fernàndez &
Fr. Thomas Anchukandam, the Former Provincial

With the CBCI President Baselios Cardinal Cleemis

With External Affairs Minister Mrs. Sushma Swaraj &
Central Minister Alphons Kannanthanam

By the Grace of God | 147

With Prime Minister Narendra Modi

With Chief Minister Pinarayi Vijayan at his Residence

With Former Chief Minister Oommen Chandy

help me–Indian Government or the Church? I don't know what they did after that."

But the uppermost feeling and emotion in me at that time was to express my deep sense of gratitude to God and to all the people who kept on praying for my well-being. This is what I told the reporters at Delhi airport: "I thank Almighty God for all that happened, the Holy Father, all the leaders of our country, the leaders of different countries and all the people for their love and concern."

Shortly after my arrival, I left for a meeting with the Honourable Prime Minister, Mr. Narendra Modi. The meeting was scheduled for 10.30 am. I was accompanied by Mr. Alphons Kannanthanam, Mr. Jose K. Mani, Mr. George Kuria-kose (Minority Commission member from Kerala), Fr. Joyce Thonikuzhiyil, Fr. Jose Mathew, and Fr. Jose Koyickal. On meeting him in his office, I offered the Prime Minister a bou-quet of flowers.

While receiving the bouquet of flowers from me, the Prime Minister held my hands and kept me close to himself and said: "Fr. Tom, welcome. How is your health? We are happy that you are here. Take care of your health now." We sat down and then I thanked him and the Government for all the efforts they had made to get me released. I told the Prime Minister that my release is the result of the prayers of so many people. In fact, my relatives told me that *poojas* were held for my release at the Ramapuram (my home town) temple and the Muslim brothers from Erattupetta offered special prayers for me.

The Prime Minister said: "Be proud of being an Indian."

Mr. Modi continued: "When you get some time please do come and share your experiences with people concerned here at Delhi so that we can have a better idea of the various operations we may be undertaking in the future." The meeting lasted about 35 minutes.

Then we went over to visit Mrs. Sushma Swaraj–the Honourable External Affairs Minister. She welcomed us with a bouquet of flowers. We exchanged the bouquets cordially. She was very happy and warm in her expressions. She held my hands and said: "We are so happy, Fr. Tom, that you are freed. You have undergone so much...and I feel sorry about that." She continued saying that when she went for the canonization of Mother Teresa in Rome, instead of five minutes the Holy Father had given her fifteen minutes to have an audience with him. While I thanked her for all the diplomatic efforts made by the Government, she expressed this in return: "I am very happy that you have come back. This was our priority. We have done our very best. For me, every citizen is important. It was very difficult to approach the abductors. Any way, we are very happy now."

Then we went to the office of the Nuncio. Archbishop Giambattista Diquattro, the ambassador of the Holy See's to India and Nepal, who came out of his office to welcome me along with the staff at the Nunciature. He then invited me for a private meeting. General V. K. Singh, the Honourable Minister of State–Ministry of External Affairs, Fr. Joyce Thonikuzhiyil, Fr. Jose Koyickal and Fr. Jose Mathew were also present at the meeting.

I thanked the Nuncio for the efforts he had made for my release. I also narrated to him my surprise meeting with the Holy Father and the situation of my health when I landed in Rome.

A typical Kerala lunch was arranged at the Nunciature. Later in the evening, the Nuncio also came for the Mass organized at the Cathedral at 6.30 pm. On the same day at 4.30 pm., a Press Meet was arranged at the CBCI centre, Delhi. The hall was packed to capacity with journalists from the national, regional and local media. The Media Secretary of CBCI acted as the moderator of the Press Meet.

Several queries were raised regarding my days of captivity and about the release. I told them: "Now I have become the property not only of my natural family, or of the Salesian family; I understand that now I belong to the entire world. God has a mission for all of us and my mission must have been to assist those sisters looking after the old and the dying."

"There is goodness in everybody; had that not been the case they would have even killed me... I feel God wants me to pray for my captors for their change of heart and for peace in the world."

One of the journalists asked me whether I have Stockholm syndrome! (It is a condition in which hostages develop a psychological alliance with their captors as a survival strategy during captivity). I replied: "People can say anything. Let those who criticize me continue to do so. I have nothing to say on that."

The Press Meet lasted for about an hour.

The next destination was the Sacred Heart Cathedral for a solemn thanksgiving Eucharist at 6.30 pm. There was an overwhelming number of people who came for the Holy Eucharist. I was very much moved when I began the celebration of the Holy Mass. I cried several times during the Mass. I couldn't control my tears when I kissed the altar at the beginning of the Mass – my first Mass in India after the captivity. The crowd was pressing around so much that I had to be whisked away from the sacristy during the recessional hymn! I have no words to thank them for their love and affection.

The dinner and the night stay was arranged at Don Bosco Provincial House, Okhla.

At the end of all these meetings, honestly, I was exhausted. But the thought of the thousands and thousands who prayed for me incessantly, making lots of personal as well as community sacrifices, made me forget even my fatigue. I have no words to express my sincere gratitude! How many generations should I live to thank you all for all what you have done for me!

What was in store for me the following day was my journey to Bangalore; to the Province where I belong. Accompanied by Fr. Joyce Thonikuzhiyil, Fr. Jose Koyickal and Fr. M.K. George, I landed in Bangalore on 29th at 8.30 am.

Mr. K. J. George, the Honourable minister for Urban Development, Karnataka, Msgr. S. Jayanathan, Rev. Fr. Antony samy, the Chancellor of the Archdiocese of Bangalore, Fr. P. S. George, the Economer of Bangalore Province, several Salesian confreres of the Province of Bangalore, Salesian

Sisters, members of the Salesian family, relatives from Ramapuram and friends were present at the airport.

From the airport we proceeded to the Provincial house where a reception was organized. After a brief period of prayer in the Chapel, I addressed the group that had gathered at the Provincial house.

At around 11am. we were on our way to St. John's Medical College, Bangalore, to meet the Cardinals and Bishops who were having the CBCI Standing Committee Meeting. I met them personally and later had lunch with them. There was also a ten-minute gathering with the doctors and staff of St. John's Medical College.

In the evening I attended a public reception held at the Good Shepherd Convention Hall, Museum Road, Bangalore. Mr. Ramalinga Reddy, the Honourable Home Minister of Karnataka was present at the gathering, besides several priests, members of the Salesian family, religious and lay faithful. There was a thanksgiving Mass on 30th at 9.30 am. with the members of the Salesian family at the Provincial house, after which there was a fraternal gathering with the Salesians. I addressed a Press Meet at 3.00 pm.

While in Bangalore, in an interview with Fr. Bobby Kannazhath sdb, the Associate Editor of Don Bosco - Salesian Magazine, I gave this message to all its readers: "My release is a proof of the power of prayer. I am grateful to all of you for your intense prayers and sacrifices for me. Let us continue to serve the Lord bereft of selfish motives. Hold on to Jesus and He will take care of us."

On Sunday, 1st October, at 6.05 am. I boarded the flight to Kochi.

I arrived at the Kochi International airport from Bengaluru around 7 am. I was received by Mr. Ramesh Chennithala, Leader of the Opposition, Jose K. Mani, MP, MLAs Hibi Eden, V. K. Ebrahim Kunju, Anwar Sadath, Roji John, and V.D. Satheesan. Mar Jacob Muricken, the Auxiliary Bishop of Pala, Mar Sebastian Vaniyapurakkal, the Curia Bishop, several Salesians, Missionaries of Charity Sisters, other religious, and a large contingent from Ramapuram were also present at the airport.

I had a breakfast stop-over at Don Bosco Cultural Centre, Vennala, Kochi. I met the people assembled there for the Sunday Mass.

Then I proceeded to the Syro-Malabar Archbishop's house. I was very affectionately received by Mar Sebastian Vaniyapurakkal, the Curia Bishop, Mar Jose Puthenveettil, the Auxilliary Bishop of Ernakulam-Angamaly Archdiocese, eminent priests of the diocese and religious. After a brief meeting with the bishops and priests at the Archbishop's house, we proceeded to the adjacent St. Mary's Cathedral Basilica at 10.30 am. I noticed that people from different walks of life had thronged there to thank God for me. A Press Meet was arranged at the Archbishop's house at 11 am.

The Archdiocese of Verapoly accorded me a warm reception at 12 noon. I was received by Archbishop Joseph Kalathiparambil. Vicars General of the Archdiocese Rev. Fr. Mathew Kallingal and Rev. Fr. Mathew Elanjimattam, along with Chancellor Rev. Fr. Ebigeen Arakkal, Mr. K. V. Thomas

MP and family were also present at the occasion. During and after lunch I spent time with the Archbishop, priests, religious and the political dignitaries present there.

Around 1.30 pm. I left for Pala where I was welcomed at the Bishop's house by Mar Joseph Pallickaparambil, Bishop emeritus of the diocese who had ordained me. During the reception I recalled 21 May 1990, when I was ordained a priest by Mar Pallickaparambil. Now I have realized that my calling is to tell the world that there is a God, who listens to our prayers and grants our requests.

My emotions ran high as I approached my home town Ramapuram. The large crowd drawn from all walks of life and religions, assembled there overwhelmed me. I was taken in procession in an open-jeep. Mr. K.M. Mani, Mr. P.J. Joseph, Mr. Thiruvanchoor Radhakrishnan, and several other political leaders and Church personnel were there to receive me. I was touched by their love and regard for me. The prayers of people right from Pope Francis to little children had sustained me.

After reaching Ramapuram I first visited the tomb of Blessed Augustine Thevarparambil (Kunjachan) inside the Chapel. This was followed by the Holy Mass and a public gathering. Then I went home where I was warmly received by my brother Mr. U.V. Mathew and my sister Mary. I felt so secure amidst my dear and near ones.

On 2nd morning at 9 am I was on my way to Vaduthala to meet the Salesian confreres of Kochi region. There was a large gathering of Salesians at Vaduthala. It was for the first time after almost three years that I could meet several of my confreres together. It was indeed a homely setting for me. The adoration service organized for the occasion by the students of Philosophy from Aluva was very heart-touching. I had enough time to interact with my confreres. There was a Press Conference in the afternoon and later at 6 pm a thanksgiving mass and a public meeting.

On the following day, at around 6.30 am I was driven to Thiruvananthapuram where I had a series of appointments. On the way I dropped in at Don Bosco Kottiyam, and had breakfast there. There was also an informal meeting with the Salesian confreres.

In Thiruvananthapuram I met the Honourable Governor of Kerala, Justice P. Sathasivam at the Raj bhavan. He was very cordial and kind. I expressed my gratitude for his intervention in ensuring my release from the terrorists. "When I received a memorandum from your family, immediately I wrote to Mrs. Sushma Swaraj, the Honourable External Affairs Minister of India," he remarked. He continued: "I want to spend more time with you in the future. I know well the Don Bosco institutions in Chennai, where I was." The Governor inquired about the political situation of Yemen and about my days in captivity. The meeting lasted about 30 minutes.

After that I called on Cardinal Baselios Mar Cleemis at the Pattom Major Archbishop's House. The Cardinal received me with great affection. There was a thanksgiving prayer service animated by the Cardinal himself! There were several priests present on the occasion. I thanked him profusely for the initiatives he had taken in his capacity as the President of CBCI.

I also visited Mr. Oommen Chandy, the former Chief Minister of Kerala, at his residence, "Puthuppally House". KPCC President M.M. Hassan, MLAs K.C. Joseph, V.S. Sivakumar, K.S. Sabarinadhan and M. Vincent were among those present. At the end of the informal meeting, I prayed with Mr. Oommen Chandy and his family members.

A short visit to Don Bosco Manacaud was a must. I celebrated Mass with the Salesian confreres. Bishop Rajendran sdb of Thuckalay Diocese was kind enough to be present there and we had an informal chat.

A formal reception was accorded to me at the Girideepam Convention Centre at Nalanchira, Thiruvananthapuram, attended by Chief Minister Mr. Pinarayi Vijayan, former Chief Minister Mr. Oommen Chandy and various religious leaders. The head of the Syro-Malankara Church, Cardinal Baselios Mar Cleemis, Trivandrum Latin Arch Diocese Auxiliary Bishop Christudas Rajappan , Marthoma Church Thiruvananthapuram Diocesan Bishop Joseph Mar Barnabas Episcopa, Palayam Imam Suhaib Moulavi, Sivagiri Mutt general secretary Swami Sandrananda and Salesian Provincial Fr. Joyce Thonikuzhiyil spoke on the occasion.

Mr. Pinarayi Vijayan, the Honourable Chief Minister of Kerala, hosted a dinner for me at his official residence, the 'Cliff House.' The dignitaries present included Cardinal Baselios Mar Cleemis, Fr. Joyce Thonikuzhiyil, Fr. Jose Koyickal, Fr. M.K. George and Fr. C.J. Sebastian. The Chief Minister was very friendly, caring and cordial.

At Don Bosco Monvila, where I went for night rest, I was warmly received by the religious of the locality as well as the Salesian Co-operators.

On the following day, 4th October, I headed towards Don Bosco Kollam. The open-jeep reception by the thousands of faithful, priests and religious who had flocked there early in the morning made a deep impact on me. The thought that I am alive today thanks to the prayers and sacrifices of such people led me to tears!

A solemn thanksgiving Eucharist was celebrated at 8am., followed by breakfast and a public gathering. Bishop Stanley Roman, Bishop of Quilon, Bishop Selvister Ponnumuthan, Bishop of Punalur, Mr. N.K. Premachandran, MP, Mr. Mukesh MLA, and several other church leaders and politicians were present. I was highly edified to see Mr. N.K. Premachandran, MP attending the whole Mass, thanking God for my release.

At 9.30 am. I proceeded to Thrissur to meet Archbishop Andrews Thazhath, the Vice-president of CBCI. On the way at Sakthikulangara I was given a warm reception by the parish priest and the faithful of the locality. After lunch at Don Bosco Angamaly, where I met the students and staff of Don Bosco Central School, I was taken to the retreat centre at Muringoor where I addressed the retreatants both at the English and Malayalam centres. The Malayalam section was having a retreat for priests attended by about 500 of them. A brief stop-over was arranged at Don Bosco College Mannuthy where I met the Salesians, staff and students of the College.

I had a very cordial meeting with Archbishop Andrews Thazhath at 4 pm at the Archbishop's house. A meeting with the priests and religious of the archdiocese was held in the auditorium, which lasted about 30 minutes. At 5 pm. a reception was arranged at Don Bosco School Mannuthy followed by a thanksgiving prayer service and a public gathering. I also paid a short visit to Mary Matha Major Seminary where I met several priests who were making their annual spiritual retreat.

After hectic days of moving around expressing my sincere gratitude to political authorities, Church leadership and people belonging to all walks of life, it was time for me to return to the Provincial House at Bangalore to recuperate. I reached Bangalore at 12.15 am on 5th October.

Though the journeys and meetings were taking a toll on my health, I had to forget about my health condition before the sincere prayerful and sacrificing attitude of thousands of people who kept on knocking at the door of heaven for me. I returned to Bangalore with a deep sense of gratitude to God Almighty and numerous individuals who played a role in getting me released. Marvellous are His ways and His mercy is immeasurable!

After returning to Bangalore on 5th I visited the Salesian Sisters at Avalahalli, and Don Bosco Technical Institute and Parish at KGF where I had worked for eight years. I was very happy to meet my former colleagues and students at the ITI.

On the following day I went to the Philomena's hospital, Bangalore to review my health. After the check-up I was found to be rather fit, without any major health problems. Thank God! My weight too had increased by 3.5 kgs. A reception was organized at the hospital along with the doctors and staff.

As I write these lines I am recuperating at Don Bosco Provincial House, Bangalore, with a few occasional visits to the formation houses of the Province. I am told that several invitations are pouring in to have me at various places – dioceses, congregations, retreat centres, churches of different Christian denominations, my Hindu brethren and even Muslim organizations! I know none of this is my merit.

However tiring or even tedious some such programmes are, I feel obliged to attend them for two reasons. First of all it is an opportunity God is presenting me with, to thank the people who so intensely prayed for me. Secondly I see it as an opportunity and my mission right now to make a personal testimony of the mercy and kindness of the Almighty who protected me and is guiding me.

A final word of sincere gratitude to everyone. Tears well up in my eyes when I think of your love and concern for me. I have nothing to give in return for all the prayers and sacrifices you have offered for my safety and release. Thanks for manifesting a new energy and a faith so vivacious and vibrant.

I am convinced that my release was the fruit of the prayers of millions worldwide, more especially, the prayers and sacrifices of my countrymen. Heartfelt thanks to each and everyone. May God bless you abundantly and recompense you as He knows best.